THE HOLY INFECTION

THE
HOLY
INFECTION

*The Mission
of the Church
in Parish and Community*

by
Paul G. Bretscher

CONCORDIA PUBLISHING HOUSE
SAINT LOUIS   LONDON

Concordia Publishing House, St. Louis, Missouri
Concordia Publishing House Ltd., London, E. C. 1
© 1969 Concordia Publishing House

Library of Congress Catalog Card No. 74-79997

MANUFACTURED IN THE UNITED STATES OF AMERICA

To my parents
Dr. and Mrs. Paul M. Bretscher

Contents

Foreword

Incisively and authoritatively, Prof. Paul G. Bretscher deals with a theme we suggested several years ago for the Institute on the Church in Mission at Concordia Seminary, St. Louis — the motif of the witnessing church as it articulates its testimony in the world through its own basic functions, notably those of service, witness, fellowship, worship and nurture.

In line with the paradoxical nature of Biblical truth, the writer is suggesting by his provocative title that Christian discipleship is caught rather than taught; and then he pivots to devote much of his stimulating text to the proposition that Christianity has to be taught if it is to be caught. With deliberate abrasiveness he insists on the need for a verbal witness to Jesus Christ and His salvation.

Amid what he regards as our vapid contemporary theological climate, Paul Bretscher harbors no illusions about the all-pervasiveness of sin and the futility of human nostrums and panaceas. But there is in him no lack of faith in the limitless power of the Word of God.

Some may disagree with the author in his reluctance to recognize both proclamation and demonstration as components of Christian witness in the world. He is stubborn and possibly even one-sided in his insistence on the indispensable character of shaping in words what God demands

11

of man and what God has done to heal him. Yet this conviction may be exactly what is needed to correct a prior one-sidedness on the part of those who imagine that people can be basically helped by silent lives of love while they avoid the scandal and discomfort of speaking the foolish Word.

This highly readable volume, at once understandable to the great majority of Christian adults and youth and challenging to any pastor and theologian, will help us face the world today with Biblical realism and with a Christian hope—a hope that rests on the power of the Word of God to use every disciple of Jesus Christ as a carrier to spread the healing contagion of Christ through a society that, corporately and individually, often fails to recognize its fatal sickness.

WILLIAM J. DANKER
Editor, The Witnessing Church Series

Introduction

The Scriptures take it for granted that the God of Israel and of the church is *different*. He stands apart from and will not be classified with anything that men call God or that they worship. The immediate consequence is that the people of this God are different too. They stand apart from and will not be like other peoples. This is the point of the great command in Lev. 19:2, "You shall be *holy*, for I the LORD your God am *holy*." We reaffirm the principle whenever we pray, "Hallowed be Thy name," and indeed whenever we confess our faith in "the *holy* Christian church, the communion of *saints*."

This differentness or "holiness" is our theme. It is vital to the church's consciousness of her nature and identity, vital also to her capacity to confront and infect a dead world with life, an enslaved world with freedom, a world of illusion with truth, a doomed world with salvation. Our task is to recover what these familiar concepts mean and to apply them to five aspects of parish life — worship, fellowship, education, service, and witness.

The terms *holiness* and *new life* depict a single reality, as the Nicene Creed implies when it calls the Holy Spirit "the Lord and Giver of life." Both holiness and life are created and sustained by God alone, the God who calls

Himself both "holy" and "living." When the church finds her holiness compromised, her life infected by the world's death, she must not "pull herself together" and by some desperate act of will rise up to do some holy things so as to prove herself alive. She must rather return to the Word of God and the Sacraments, listen, be comforted, eat and drink heartily, learn from God again what her holiness and life really is, and receive it freely and joyfully as a gift. Only then can she do her work with joy rather than under the burden of shame and self-accusation.

For the counterinfection of death is always with us and in us as long as God chooses to leave us in this world. The whole history of God's people testifies to that. What God intends His people to be is clear enough, for example, in the segment of Law from Lev. 17 to 26, which scholars have called the "Holiness Code." "You shall be holy to Me; for I the LORD am holy and have separated you from the peoples, that you should be Mine," says Lev. 20:26. The code illustrates in many ways how their differentness from the Canaanites is to show. They are not to participate in the sexual abominations that the Canaanites practice by religious sanction, or run to mediums and wizards to try to foresee and thus control their own future, or pursue their own advantage at the expense of others by theft, oppression, or treachery. The Law commands an open-handed generosity and love, extending not only to the neighbor but also to the stranger in the land. For all they have, including the land itself, is theirs freely as the gift of God, the inheritance from the LORD who brought them out of Egypt. But if they "walk in the customs of the nation" that the LORD is casting out before them (Lev. 20:23), they "profane the name" of their God (18:21) and "defile" themselves (18:24). In that case the land will vomit them out also. (18:28)

The history of Israel testifies continually to the failure of their holiness. The Holiness Code promised life to the people if they kept God's statutes and ordinances (Lev. 18:5; cf. Luke 10:28), but the infection of death prevailed. Ezek. 36−37 tells how the nation "died" as the land vomited them out in the Babylonian exile. They had defiled the land by their unholy ways (Ezek. 36:17), and profaned God's holy name (36:20). The nations were drawing the inference that the LORD, the God of Israel, had Himself failed them and been conquered just as other gods of other cities and lands had been conquered. Therefore, Ezekiel promises, the LORD will act to vindicate the holiness of His great name (36:23) by cleansing the people from their uncleanness, giving them a new heart and spirit, and restoring them to their land (36:24-32). According to the great parable of Ezek. 37, the LORD by His Spirit will raise the dead bones of Israel from their graves and by returning them to their land restore them to life.

The struggle for holiness is reflected again in the era of Jesus and St. Paul. Judaism was characterized by a vital concern to maintain its holiness, to be distinct from the nations by way of genealogy, circumcision, foods, Sabbath, and other laws, including those we think of as moral. Yet Jesus sees how an unholy infection has made their very holiness unclean (Matt. 12:43-45). Though they claim to be righteous under the Law, they are deeply offended when the mercy of God overflows freely and without legal conditions to repentant apostates like tax collectors and harlots. This exposes their unholiness, for they defend their superior righteousness even to the point of bypassing the wounded and dying sinner. How can they then claim to have kept the Law, to have loved their neighbor as themselves (Luke 10:25-37)? They call themselves sons of the Father, and rightly so (see Ex. 4:22-23). Yet sons are to reflect the Father. If the Father "makes the sun rise on the evil and on the good, and sends rain on the just and on the unjust," it is a contradiction in terms for His sons to love and greet only those who love and greet them. The differentness of the sons of God from sinners and Gentiles shows in their capacity to love even their enemies, and thus to be "perfect, as their heavenly Father is perfect" (Matt. 5:43-48), or as Luke 6:36 has it: "Be merciful, even as your Father is merciful."

St. Paul pursues the theme. It is not enough to have the Law and to boast of it, he says. Not the hearers but the doers shall be justified (Rom. 2:13). His diagnosis of the best of Judaism in his day picks up the theme of Ezek. 36, "The name of God is blasphemed among the Gentiles because of you" (Rom. 2:24). As the identity of God's people has passed from Judaism through Christ to the church, so now the call to holiness is the church's call. In Gal. 5:16-24 St. Paul draws the sharp contrast between the "works of the flesh" and the "fruit of the Spirit." The latter includes "love, joy, peace, patience, kindness, goodness, faithfulness, gentleness, self-control." These characterize the new life of holiness and freedom. "Do not be conformed to this world but be transformed by the renewal of your mind," the apostle says in Rom. 12:2. To the Thessalonians he says: "The Lord make you increase and abound in love . . . that He may establish your hearts unblamable in holiness before our God and Father." (1 Thess. 3:12-13; see 4:1-8)

These are all familiar texts. Yet as we look out on the life of any parish we know, what cause have we to believe that the performance of those whom the Collect calls "Christ's holy people" is any great improvement over that of Old Testament Israel? The holy infection is supposed to be working into an unholy world through us. The power of life is supposed to penetrate and repel the death. Light

16

is to dissipate the darkness. Yet the reverse seems to be happening. Death infects the life. The world invades the church and conforms it to itself. All the old indictments against the failure of Israel ring so very true in our own ears. What has happened to the holy infection? Dare we still pray, "Hallowed be Thy name," we who are so constantly guilty of profaning that very name?

Yes, we dare, and we can, and we must. That is our great advantage. For all our failure, we can look back to one place, one eternally precious moment when holiness was fulfilled. For there was a Man among us, whose name we now bear, who lived out the holiness of His Father's name and exhibited without ambiguity, in the concreteness of this earth, the glaring contrast between holiness and unholiness, between life and death. Strange, how lonely that climactic moment was for Jesus! His disciples had fled in fear and despair. The "holy" nation of Israel had conspired with the unholy Gentiles to charge Him with blasphemy against God's name and to put Him to death as the enemy of God and of the emperor. No moment reveals the pain and the power of holiness as that moment does. The cross is unclean, the epitome of disgrace, defilement, death. Yet we are compelled to wreathe that cross and Him who hangs there with a *halo* — not first of all because of His deity but because *holiness* had its fulfillment there, in Him. This is the holy Son of the holy Father, the Son who hallows the Father's name in deed and in truth. In the face of the shame and terror of the cross, He says, "I will" to the cup the Father gives Him to drink, "I will' to the call to love neighbor and stranger and enemy as Himself. That is why the Resurrection points the world to the moment of its greatest shame and abhorrence and says, "*There* is holiness!" And if we do not see holiness there, there will be no holiness for us, no infection of life in a world of death. This is the turning point of holiness in an unholy world.

Therefore everything we shall say about holiness must proceed from and constantly return to that moment. Only by reference to that moment can we or anyone pray, "Hallowed be Thy name." In Jesus that prayer has already been answered. (John 12:28)

1

In the Cacophony of Men — Quiet and a Hallelujah (Worship)

The very term *holiness* implies a contrast, we are saying, because to be holy is to be different. The difference shows first in the worship of God's people. The point is not that God's people worship and others do not. Everybody worships. But Christian worship stands out from and against every other worship. It is different. Only in its differentness can it be a salt in the raw wounds of the world, a light in its darkness, a holy infection.

Luther was very perceptive at this point. In the Large Catechism definition of the First Commandment he says: "A god is that to which we look for all good and in which we find refuge in every distress." The definition is broad enough to allow for no atheism. As long as men look for good somewhere or find ways to flee from evil, they have a god. The very activity of seeking the good from their god and fleeing the evil by his help — that activity is their worship. Likewise the joy men experience when their pursuit is successful and they get what they want or escape the danger they fear — that joy or relief expresses their worship. And still again, the bitterness, anger, frustration, and hatred men exhibit when their desires are thwarted and their devices fail — that too belongs to their worship. For they invoke their gods and curse the world and its injustice. All this is nothing less than worship.

So I suggest that the worship of men is dramatized in cacophony, in strident noises. I don't want to overdo this point. Not all noises need necessarily be included. The roar of a crowd at a ball game, the sound of an orchestra or a chorus, the thunder of a stamping machine in a factory — leave these out of it. But there are certain noises that intrigue me for the hidden quality of worship they express — for example, some popular music. Why it has to be so loud, why it must assault the senses so persistently and repetitiously, and why my children go for it — that mystifies me. Perhaps such music expresses an inner fear of not being heard, of not being noticed. If so, it belongs to worship, to the cacophony with which Christian worship stands in contrast. Or again, it is curious to me that many songs these days do not end. They trail off into nothing, as though the listener is to keep singing. And I wonder whether this too does not express the mood of the world's worship — the fear of ending, the awareness that the great creative enterprise of man lasts for so short a moment, the dread of being forgotten. If so, it belongs to the noise that contrasts with Christian worship. Such noise cannot say amen. Rather it resists and fears the notion that "the end of all things is at hand," and regards that as a great evil.

The idea that the noises men make tell something about their worship is signaled in Ex. 32. Moses and Joshua come down from the mountain and are first attracted by strange noises. Joshua thinks it is the sound of war, but to Moses it sounds like dancing and singing. It is worship. The people have despaired of God, because for 40 days they have seen no sign of Him or of Moses. Therefore they have resorted to their own devices and fashioned a god who is at least as valuable as the gold they have invested in the calf — a real and tangible god who will be there when they want to see him, and not leave them so desperately alone for 40 days. But to have a god is to celebrate him and expect things from him. Such celebration and expectation calls for activity, and the activity is worship.

So listen for the noises, and ask whether they do not express a kind of worship. Listen to people arguing and damning each other. Hear the cry of mobs, their vandalism and violence, their anger and looting, their delight in the fires they set. It is all a form of worship. Listen to the sound of guns, in cities as well as in warfare. Listen to the bombs, to the artillery and rocket attacks, to the lists of wounded and dead, to the charges and countercharges of anger and frustration, to the terror and the tears, the emptiness of the lost and refugees who have no place to go. Is not that too a worship? Listen to the protests, the accusations and the denials, the demands and the resistance to demands, the silent marches and the violent ones. Listen to the men who count themselves wise and responsible, who know the answers, who call for investigations and panels and legislation and spending. Is not all this, too, the noise of worship? Or hear the exultant boasts in the achievements of science and engineering, the courageous "Carry on!" after the fiery deaths of three astronauts, the promises of a more glorious future. Or listen to someone sob in despair at the loss of all beauty and security and meaning, to someone paralyzed by an overpowering sense of the futility of man, to someone crying and yet unable to cry—that too is a worship. Even the silent sound of suicide has the quality of worship about it.

For worship is the response man makes in his pursuit of good and his flight from evil. Luther's definition, "A god is that to which we look for all good and in which we take refuge from all distress" answers remarkably to the description of sin in the story of the Fall, that man wants to be "wise, like God, knowing good and evil." In his little book

Creation and Fall, Dietrich Bonhoeffer offers an exegesis of the knowledge of good and evil that to me is very fruitful and persuasive. To know good and evil is to distinguish between *pleasure* and *pain,* he says in effect. But this becomes at one and the same time the distinction between *passion* and *hate,* for once man has distinguished between what will give him pleasure and what will hurt him, he pursues with passion the thing he has decided is good, and he flees from and hates what he thinks is evil.[1] Note this definition well. Except in rare instances when I clearly specify otherwise, I shall be assuming it throughout this book. *Good* and *evil* are not moral terms here, as when we speak of good and evil men. *Good* and *evil* denote what any man whose eyes have been "opened" (Gen. 3:6-7) judges to be advantageous or disadvantageous to him.

Luther himself did not interpret "the tree of knowledge of good and evil" this way, and so failed to tie it to his definition of the First Commandment. Yet he had a remarkable grasp of the concept. In the Heidelberg Disputation he observes how the theologian of glory ends up calling evil good and good evil, whereas the theologian of the cross calls a thing what it really is.[2] In effect the theologian of the cross leaves the knowledge of good and evil to God. Adam is a perfect example of the glory theologian. The best thing that happened on the evening of the Fall was that the LORD God came into the garden. Yet Adam thought this good thing was evil, and ran to hide. The worst thing that could happen was that the man would try to deceive God rather than throw himself on God's mercy. Yet to Adam this worst thing seemed to be the good, and he did it. He knew good and evil all right!

Thus every man by nature assumes that it is his responsibility to keep his eyes wide open so as to distinguish what will be good and bad for him. To become wiser is to become more capable of refining one's distinctions. To be mature means to recognize that we sometimes can't have the good without a measure of evil. There may be pain and fear in the dentist's chair, but we grit our teeth and submit to it in pursuit of a greater good. The costs of war may escalate and frustration mount to despair, but wise men have argued that the evil must be borne for the sake of the greater good or to prevent an even greater evil. Even the assassin operates by the knowledge of good and evil. What he does seems good to him. The arsonist, the looter of burning stores, and the man who incites riots, as well as the man whose prescription for social ills is more and better policemen — all are pursuing what they think is good and resisting what they think is evil.

To know good and evil is to be godlike. To act on the knowledge in order to determine one's best possible future is to worship and serve that god. But all the wars and fightings and clashes of man with man, all of man's struggle to make something of himself and get ahead, all the boasting on the one hand and the hatred and fear and cursing on the other — all these things exhibit man in the process of worshiping the god by whom he seeks to have the good and avoid the evil.

The contrast to which the holy God calls His holy people and which His people exhibit in their worship is glaring indeed. For the people of God are conformed to the image of Christ. They are not "wise," they are not "like God," and they don't "know good and evil." That is the point of Jesus' prayer in Matt. 11:25-26: "I thank Thee, Father, Lord of heaven and earth, that Thou hast hidden these things from the wise and understanding and revealed them to babes; yea, Father, for such was Thy gracious will."

The "wise and understanding" were, in Jesus' case, men like the Pharisees and rabbis. The Pharisees exhibited their wisdom and understanding by the way they calculated consequences. They kept their eyes open. They would not believe that the kingdom of heaven was at hand unless they could see a sign from heaven. They were concerned, because they had advantages in this practical life that they did not want to let go without some concrete assurance that the gains or rewards would more than compensate for the losses. That was their knowledge of good and evil at work. That's why they made excuses. One had just married a wife, another had bought a field and another five yoke of oxen (Luke 14:18-20). What an awkward time for the kingdom of heaven to arrive! What they really could not give up was not so much these things, however, as their *wisdom and prudence,* their knowledge of good and evil.

It was by his knowledge of good and evil that the Pharisee compared himself to the tax collector and expected a very high place at the banquet table (Luke 14:7-11). He couldn't surrender his bargaining position and superior right. He could not let go of his control of the future. He couldn't trust God with the seating arrangements, for what if some miserable tax collector were assigned a place ahead of him? Thus the mercy of God seemed evil, the justice of God seemed good. Or what if he did not receive proper recognition and credit for his superior loyalty to the Law? No, the Pharisee trusted his knowledge of good and evil, and not God. That is why he couldn't "see" Jesus and what God was doing and saying were hid from him.

The disciples weren't much better. They too were worried about seating arrangements. The fact that they had left everything behind to follow Christ ought to entitle them to superior positions, they thought. But then they began to argue among themselves who would be the *most* superior. That was when Jesus had to set a baby before them and insist that the disciples become like this child; otherwise they would never make it into the Kingdom (Matt. 18:1-4). Nobody can get into the Kingdom who does not park his weapons at the door, who does not abandon the wisdom of knowing good and evil! A child doesn't know. That is his beauty.

In Deut. 1 Moses rehearses the history of Israel at Kadesh-barnea and their response to the report of the 12 spies. They had thought that to enter the Promised Land would be good, that to stay in the wilderness was evil, that to be slaves in Egypt was the worst condition of all. But when they heard about the walled cities and the weapons of war and the giants, they went into panic. They knew good and evil! "We will all be slaughtered!" they cried. "Our wives and little children will be the helpless prey of the ruthless enemy! The Promised Land is evil," they decided, "and Egypt is good! We should never have left Egypt!" they said. "Moses is a terrible leader, and God is a stupid God!" That response was worship, but its very noise of hatred, fear, and complaint exhibited all too well what god they were worshiping. So the judgment fell. Not one of those adult, mature, wise people who knew good and evil would make it into the land! All would perish in the wilderness.

But those little ones, Moses says, "who you said would become a prey, and your children, who this day *have no knowledge of good or evil,* shall go in there, and to them I will give [the land], and they shall possess it" (Deut. 1:39). The children played in the sand while all the argument and weeping was going on. They had no fear of the giants and the weapons of war. They would go wherever their parents, wherever the LORD took them. Thus it was a childlike people, a people without the knowledge of good and evil, a people who could trust God to know good and evil for them — that kind of people crossed the Jordan and walked around the walls of Jericho and received the land. Joshua and Caleb went in with them, for at Kadesh only these two, among all the adults, forsook the calculating wisdom of the world for the sake of the wisdom of faith in the promises of God. And so Jesus also declares: "Unless you turn and become like children, you will never enter the kingdom of heaven." (Matt. 18:3)

Here, in the giving up of the knowledge of good and evil, lies the beginning and the end of the knowledge and worship of the living God. In his definition of the First Commandment in the Small Catechism, Luther draws together three terms for worship of God that pervade the whole Old Testament, the terms *fear, love,* and *trust.* "We should fear, love, and trust God above all things." There is no higher worship than this, for worship at its best means taking God at His word and letting Him be God. But notice the sharp antithesis between this worship of God and the worship implied by the knowledge of good and evil. To *fear God* means *not to fear evil,* not to cringe from obedience in the face of evil and threat, as Israel did at Kadesh (compare Matt. 10:28). To *love God* means *not to love good,* as those covetous wise men did who offered excuses because they valued the new wife or field or oxen above the promise of the kingdom of God (Luke 14:18-20). To *trust in God* means *not* to rely on one's own insight (Prov. 3:5), that is, on one's private ability to decide and anticipate what will be good or bad for one. All such calculation must be left behind if the true God is to be worshiped. For man worships God when he ceases to distinguish between good and evil, between advantage and disadvantage, but receives his life from God. Then he does not compare himself with other men, either in jealousy of those above him or in condescending satisfaction over those beneath him. He does not know good or evil. All he knows is God, and that is enough! St. Paul understood it: "All things work together for good to them that love God." (Rom. 8:28)

The Scriptures are loaded with this theme. Polytheistic religion always distinguishes between good and evil, ascribing good to one god and evil to another. Baal was the god of rain, hence of life to the Canaanites. He was the source of good. But Mot was the god of death and the source of evil. The Scriptures constantly repudiate that kind of distinction. Both life and death come from God. David would rather commit himself and his people to the direct wrath of God in a plague than choose some experience of evil that might conceivably derive from a source other than God (2 Sam. 24:14). Job says to his wife: "Shall we receive good at the hand of God, and shall we not receive evil?" (Job 2:10). In the remarkable Ps. 131 the abandonment of human wisdom concerning good and evil is described as a return to childhood:

O LORD, my heart is not lifted up,
   my eyes are not raised too high;
I do not occupy myself with things
   too great and too marvelous for me.
But I have calmed and quieted my soul,
   like a child quieted at its mother's breast;
   like a child that is quieted is my soul.
O Israel, hope in the LORD
   from this time forth and forevermore.

Because "darkness is as light with Thee" (Ps. 139:12), the child of God can walk with his Shepherd through the valley of the shadow of death and fear no evil. (Ps. 23)

Thus worship among God's people opposes the cacophony of men with quiet and a hallelujah. "Be still and know that I am God" (Ps. 46). "Fear not, stand firm,

27

and see the salvation of the LORD. . . . The LORD will fight for you, and you have only to be still," says Moses at the Red Sea. (Ex. 14:13-14)

Or look at the Book of Habakkuk. The situation was desperate when Habakkuk wrote. The joy over the collapse of Assyria had been dissipated by the tragic defeat and death of Josiah and the predatory lust for conquest exhibited by Assyria's successor, Babylon. The peace and freedom that seemed to be good was quickly torn away, and evil loomed more fearfully than ever. Nobody could understand where God was, why He didn't act, or what He was doing. Yet, Habakkuk says, Hang on! Wait! "The righteous shall live by his faith" (Hab. 2:4). And he climaxes his message with the great sentence, "The LORD is in His holy temple; let all the earth keep silence before Him" (Hab. 2:20). In what looks to your opened eyes like evil, *be quiet!* In the experience of good, shout, "Hallelujah!" That is the worship of the children of God.

The question arises, of course, how such knowledge of God ever began. And if, in the face of overwhelming evil, faith begins to fail, where shall a man look to see and know God? For to worship the living God, His people must know that He lives. They must know Him. How do they get this remarkable knowledge? As we face this question, we become aware that true worship, unlike the cacophonous worship of those who know good and evil, is not initiated by man. It has its beginning in God. It is always only a response to God. For that reason the place to look for God is not up, or ahead in the future somewhere, or around in the natural world somewhere, but *back*—back into the history of what God has said and done.

This is the point, I think, of that remarkable little episode between Moses and the Lord recorded in Ex. 33: 12-23. In the background of this text is the story of the golden calf. The people have sinned, been chastised, and been forgiven. Now it is time to face ahead, into a hard and uncertain future. Moses does not ask God whether the life ahead of him and his people will be good or evil. The distinctness of God's people, the sign of God's favor to them, lies not in some superior glory or riches Yahweh may give them but solely in the fact that He, their God, is *present* with them. "Is it not in Thy going with us . . . that we are distinct, I and Thy people, from all other people that are upon the face of the earth?" (Ex. 33:16)

When the LORD now promises that He will indeed be present with them, Moses asks to see God's glory. The LORD agrees that He will make His goodness pass before Moses and will proclaim before him His name, "Yahweh." But one thing is impossible, says the LORD, namely that Moses should look God in the face, for that would kill him. What this means is that Moses cannot be allowed to see God *coming toward him*. He can see God only after God has passed by. As He comes toward Moses and while He is passing by, the LORD keeps Moses covered with His hand. But when He has finished passing by, He removes His hand, and Moses sees the glory of God from the rear. He sees the *posteriora dei*, as Luther refers to this by way of the Vulgate in the Heidelberg Theses.[3] He sees the backside of God.

The knowledge of the true God is possible only by looking back. That is why man in his knowledge of good and evil simply cannot know God. For under the knowledge of good and evil man must face forward, ahead, toward the future, ultimately toward death. Here is the final irony of knowing good and evil—that as you look ahead the only certainty you have is that you will die! So why do we want to know good and evil? We want to know it so that we can control events and adjust our actions in order to create for ourselves a better future. We want to do the thing *now* that will prove to our best advantage tomorrow. That is what human wisdom is all about. But such wisdom means facing forward. We look back only to gather a few evidences out of past experience that may help us in our next round of calculation. The gambler looks at the dope sheets, and they are the story of past performance. But he looks at them so that he may make the wisest decision now, so that the future outcome may be for him good and not evil!

Thus if sinful man ever does look for God, what he is looking for is some force that will support him in the private distinctions he makes between good and evil and in the devices he employs to achieve the one and avoid the other. It was just such a desire to probe the future and secure the help of the gods for good that drove the Canaanites to diviners, augurers, soothsayers, sorcerers, wizards, necromancers, etc. (Deut. 18:9-14). But the God of the Bible just will not be that kind of God. If any man insists that God conform to his private terms and specifications, the confrontation with God as God is will only paralyze him with fear, drive him to despair, and kill him.

God does indeed come out of the future into the present, but He will not allow us to look for Him in that direction. If we want to see Him, we must look back and see Him after He has gone by. The look at the backside of God is implied in the whole of Biblical theology and in the whole worship of God's people. God reveals His name to Moses, "Yahweh" or "the LORD." But that name is immediately filled with content by past events. "I am Yahweh your God, who brought you out of the land of Egypt," says the preface to the Ten Commandments. "You shall have no other gods before Me" (Ex. 20:2-3). So also in the Holiness Code the constant refrain is "I am Yahweh" or "I am Yahweh your God" or, in its fullest form, "I am Yahweh your God, who brought you out of the land of Egypt." (Lev. 19:36 and context)

But to look at God in this way requires forsaking the knowledge of good and evil. When you look *back* to see God, you *do not ask* any more what the future will bring. The future will become present by *the will of God* and according to *His* purpose and promise. You know only that you were a nation of slaves in cruel bondage, yet you see now that even this was by the will of God. You know that God delivered you, that He came and saw and remembered and acted and delivered you by promise even when you were afraid and rebellious, and that He gave you the land. It is the past history that guarantees your security in the future. *Remember* what God did, and then you will not fear to follow Him!

Always the look is to the past. Behind Egypt stand the promises made to the patriarchs, Abraham, Isaac, and Jacob. Behind the patriarchs stands the God who in the beginning created the heaven and the earth. That is as far as man can look. He cannot go behind the beginning or speculate about God's thoughts. He can know God only by what God has said. He can only see how God in the past has again and again spoken to His people. Out of that past comes the Word to the present, and the relief of anxiety for tomorrow.

In their worship the people of Israel always looked at the backside of God. The man who brings the sacrifice of firstfruits, according to Deut. 26, remembers the past. He recalls the "wandering Aramean" who was his father. He recites the sojourn and bondage in Egypt, the deliverance by "a mighty hand and an outstretched arm," the entrance into Canaan and the possession of the "land flowing with milk and honey." This past determines his present act of worship. He brings the very first of the crop to the LORD, for the knowledge of God he has by looking into and remembering the past is all the security he needs that the rest of the crop will indeed grow and mature and that the future, though invisible to him, is secure in the hand of God. This is his joy, and it overflows in liberality. All the great feasts were celebrated by looking at the backside of God. However distant that past seemed to be, the look and the celebration bridged the time and made the old event always contemporary. As Ps. 90 puts it, "LORD, Thou hast been our dwelling place in all generations."

Therefore the great sin and the beginning of all apostasy is to "forget" what God has done. The moment such a forgetting occurs, faith vanishes (Ps. 78:11, 22). That is why Moses earnestly warns Israel against the great peril of prosperity. Moses fears that when they enjoy the blessings of the land, they will forget the LORD their God, who brought them out of Egypt, and begin to imagine that they have what they have by their own power (Deut. 8:11-20). But the moment they forget, they will begin to find their God somewhere else than by looking at the backside of His words and acts. Thus they will become exactly what the other nations are, and like these they too will perish.

This way of seeing the glory of God by looking at Him from the back is reflected also in texts that describe faith as a waiting. When the times are filled with crises, and events look terrifying, then the temptation looms large to resort to the knowledge of good and evil. We have mentioned Habakkuk's call to *wait* and *be silent* in the face of the Babylonian threat. Another instance would be the peril of Ahaz and Jerusalem when the alliance of Syria and Ephraim threatened to overrun Jerusalem. Ahaz reacted out of the knowledge of good and evil. His strategy was to save himself by inviting Assyria to attack his petty opponents from their rear. Isaiah called for faith rather than strategy. Let happen what will happen, Isaiah urged. The opposing kings are only men, but Yahweh is King of Jerusalem. "If you will not believe, surely you shall not be established" (Is. 7:9). Or there is the great story of Jeremiah, who summons the rulers of Judah to surrender their city and their own lives to the Babylonians and in the midst of disaster to trust the promises (Jer. 38). Or there is Ps. 27:14: "Wait for the LORD; be strong, and let your heart take courage; yea, wait for the LORD!"

The point is always that when the dark clouds are overhead and disaster looms, the people of God cannot know good and evil. In the midst of trouble they cannot understand what God has in mind for them. The hand of God covers them in the cleft of the rock while God is going by. It is a time for quiet and for prayer. But when it is done, if they will only wait in quiet and let God do what He will, then they will understand and know God. They will see Him from the rear, but they will see His glory, His mercy, His faithfulness, the marvel of His purpose.

Christian worship too has the quality of a look out of the cleft of the rock at the backside of God. That is how the glory of God is to be seen and how God is to be known. Thus as Jesus approached His Passion, the disciples were filled with fear and foreboding. In their desire for good and their fear of evil they could not stop looking ahead. What they wanted to see was God coming in glory, God straddling the Mount of Olives (Zech. 14:4), God in a sign of transcendent splendor turning the powers of this world upside down and giving Israel the Kingdom. They wanted the 12 legions of angels to multiply a thousandfold the power of their own petty swords. It was impossible for them, as long as they looked ahead, to see good in any other terms, not even when Jesus tried to tell them.

So Jesus could only commit them to the care of His

Father (John 17), and the Father in turn kept them in the cleft of the rock, in the darkness, able to see and understand nothing. To them no moment of history was more evil, more empty, more guilty, more filled with injustice, more terrifying than this moment when their Jesus hung helpless, crucified. It seemed that God was dead, for Jesus had utterly committed Himself in faith to the Father, and yet God did not act! It seemed that all the promises of the Kingdom were dead. The whole religion was dead. For if *Jesus* was not of the truth, if His faith turned out to be nothing but illusion, if God's promises proved to be empty, then there was no place left to go. So dark and full of fear was their world!

But suddenly the hand of God was lifted from the cleft of the rock, and they could come up and look around. The tomb was empty; Jesus had risen! He said, "Peace" and, "Don't be afraid," and showed them His hands and side (John 20). He breathed His Spirit on them, the Spirit of truth, who would guide them into all the truth.

Now they began to understand. They had tried to know good and evil, and God had killed their knowledge of good and evil. What they saw now was the glory of what God had done. For if the kingdom of God had come as they wanted it, it would have been the death of all the unrighteous and sinners of the world. Salvation was for the righteous, but by now it was clear that there were no righteous! All were exposed as sinners. Not only the Gentiles were sinners, not only the harlots and tax collectors, but also the Pharisees and the priests, yes, and Jesus' own disciples. No one was righteous, not one! The kingdom John the Baptist proclaimed arrived, but when it came it only exposed the whole world in its evil and ungodliness. There was only one true Son of God, only one righteous man, only one who loved God with all His heart, soul, strength, and mind, and His neighbor as Himself! That was Jesus. But the Father summoned Jesus to throw Himself in between — as Moses had once wanted to throw himself in between (Ex. 32:31-34), as the Suffering Servant was described as doing (Is. 53) — "to give His life as a ransom for many" (Matt. 20:28). Jesus drank the cup of wrath that, according to Jer. 25:15-29, all nations would have to drink. He walked to the cross in defiance of man's knowledge of good and evil. The kingdom of God came at that very moment, on the Hill of the Skull. But Jesus swallowed that terrible day of the wrath and judgment against the whole world, swallowed it in His own death.

That's why the earth had to shake and the veil be torn. That's why the promise of the Kingdom and dominion over all kingdoms that had been spoken to Israel as a people could be realized in only this one Man. He rose, and God highly exalted Him to His own right hand and gave Him the name above every name. And God said: "You cannot call that Friday evil any more. When you come out of the cleft of the rock, you must call it good, the day of the greatest and eternal manifestation of the glory of God, the day the Kingdom came and the cross became a throne and the crown of thorns the crown of glory." "You don't know good and evil," God said on that day. "The knowledge of good and evil is Mine, and Mine alone!"

And God said: "If you want to know Me, don't look for Me anywhere except in Jesus Christ crucified. Don't try to look into the future and see Me, for you will find there only your dreams and illusions. When I break them down and make you face reality, you will see only darkness and despair, wrath and death. Don't try to look up to heaven and see Me, or into your philosophy or into your psychology or into your study of the world's religions."

God says: "If you want to know Me, you must know

35

Me in the person of Jesus Christ crucified, and nowhere else. That is where you will know what mercy and forgiveness is, and how you can be My people in spite of everything. But if you know Me there," says God, "you will have to die to your old self. The man that wants to be wise, to be like God, knowing good and evil, must die; that old Adam which is your former nature must die. And the new man will be made in the image of Christ, in the likeness of His resurrection."

That is what we celebrate in our worship. Whatever belongs to worship, whether Baptism or Lord's Supper or preaching, it always reveals to us again the backside of God, the glory of the Cross. Our baptism is a past event. We can only remember and look back on it. But the name of the Father and of the Son and of the Holy Ghost in our baptism carries us right back to the moment of history when the Kingdom came in that one man and when the world was saved from wrath through Him. We eat the Lord's Supper now, in remembrance of Him who fulfilled the Passover by giving His body and shedding His blood for us. And no preaching is Christian preaching that does not proclaim and reveal God in terms of what He has done in that great event.

Christian worship sets us in the middle of time. The effect is remarkable. We look back and know God there in His forgiving mercy. But that vision releases us from attachment to anything else in the past. If what we are is determined by the Word of God, if we are sons of God by baptism into Christ, then all the guilt that may rise up out of yesterday to accuse us has nothing to say either. So also our petty successes, which might tempt us to exalt ourselves and receive congratulations for our superiority, are also past and have nothing to say. There is only one past that is normative for us, and that is the glory of God revealed to us not in the terrifying face of a God coming toward us in radiant glory but in the backside of God, which we see in the face of the man Christ Jesus. And if we have passed through personal crises and pains, and these are now past for us, such experiences too get their whole meaning from the God who now lets us see how He was there all the time, turning what seemed evil to good for us and for others. (Gen. 50:20; Rom. 8:28)

As for the future, this too belongs to God. Ahead lies the promise of resurrection for our bodies and of Christ's coming to receive us as His people and body to Himself, to share His eternal reign. When that will be, what the form of it will be, does not concern us. It is God's business, and we can wait and hope in Him. As for the more immediate future, like tomorrow, we need not grasp for that either. The Lord Jesus teaches us to pray, "Give us this day our daily bread." The prayer is reminiscent of the manna in the wilderness, when Israel had to live one day at a time, receiving the gift anew each morning. "Do not be anxious about tomorrow," says Jesus, but let tomorrow worry about itself (Matt. 6:34). There is a great freedom! The Father, who gives all gifts and is our Refuge in every distress, takes responsibility for our tomorrow. We don't have to calculate proudly and fearfully for our best advantage, out of the knowledge of good and evil. All that old wisdom is dead once we know the God and Father of our Lord Jesus Christ.

So what we have is *today*. And today is full of the presence of our God (Ex. 33:14-15; Matt. 28:20). Today is ours, to seize the life He gives and use it to His glory. Today is the time to worship, to remember God and thus to see Him everywhere and in everything, the Giver of all good gifts. And if today is dark and the threat of evil looms against us, we can bear it in watchful waiting and prayer. We don't have to know good and evil as long as God knows, the God who in His Son has conquered for us even the last evil, death. Read Heb. 12:11 again: "For the moment [while it is happening] all discipline seems painful rather than pleasant [evil rather than good]; later [when God's hand is lifted and we see His glory from behind] it yields the peaceful fruit of righteousness to those who have been trained by it."

Thus the people of God are holy, different, separate from the world. They live within the cacophony; they experience their full measure of suffering, even unjust suffering. Often they suffer willingly what the world would readily escape and evade. But even this belongs to the unique quality of their worship. Their worship answers to the God they know and trust and serve. In darkness, threat, and trouble they know that the hand of God is covering them as He passes by. Therefore they put aside their proud and vain questions and find *quiet* in God, like a child on its mother's breast. And when the darkness lifts, they see the good gifts of God pouring out on them in riches beyond all deserving and expectation. Therefore the sounds they make belong to the harmony of the new song of God's holy people, and the refrain is a joyful "Hallelujah!" They are, in fact, a hallelujah people.

Because they are that, they are an infection of holiness and life at work in the body of a humanity that is corrupt and evil and doomed to death.

2

In the Fragmentation of Men — The Family of God (Fellowship)

The church as a holy people of God, in the fellowship of Christ, acts as a holy infection toward the healing of a divided humanity. I do not deny the existence of effective societies among men but only magnify again the contrast of holiness. For it is only as the church is different from the world that it can be a salt and a light, an infection of life in a body of death.

The fact is that the knowledge of good and evil has power to unite men as well as to divide them. It unites men whenever they perceive that it is to their common advantage to be united. It divides them whenever the loss involved in such unity seems to outweigh the gain.

Thus, for example, Eve was very considerate and sociable after she had eaten the fruit (Gen. 3). She immediately gave some to Adam. And when both had fallen, they still had strong reasons for continuing as a society of sorts. When God came walking into their garden, it was to their common advantage to hide from Him. They both held their breath, and neither betrayed the other. And their social cooperation was evident in the fact that both came out wearing fig leaves — the first "Mr. and Mrs." costumes. Whichever one had the idea first shared it quickly with the other. And when the LORD had left them again after that terrible scene, I wonder whether Adam did not perhaps turn to Eve and say to her, "Personally, Honey, I thought you looked pretty good in that outfit," to which she may have replied, "You didn't look so bad yourself." In such mutual consolation they wouldn't have to worry too much anymore about what God thought. At least they had each other.

For there is a common conspiracy among men that we will accept each other in our fig leaves, that we will take one another at face value, that we will be impressed by excellence of appearance, that we will not search out hypocrisies. We do it for the other fellow on the assumption he will do it for us. Since we know what it means to be embarrassed, we help the other fellow cover up his embarrassment. We do not expose his shame to public view. Thus the knowledge of good and evil makes a cooperative society possible.

In a sense we may say that God Himself very artfully uses man's knowledge of good and evil to keep a corrupt world going. If you don't *love* your neighbor, you at least find it advantageous to treat him decently. And if some rogue comes in to disrupt things, then you join with the good guys to restrain the bad guy who threatens everybody. So we have government. Order is good, chaos is evil, and everybody must behave. We also cooperate economically, for we are more and more dependent on what the other fellow produces. And as the world becomes smaller and communications speed up and the population grows and everybody knows within 24 hours what everybody else is doing, the knowledge of good and evil demands decisions and programs and devices to keep the whole of international humanity from drifting into havoc and chaos. Every organization of society grows out of the desire of men to have for themselves the greatest possible good and to avoid or overcome the evil.

But this same force works also to produce oppressions and disruptions among men. For the man who is wise, like

God, distinguishing good and evil, is the center of his own world, and the strategy of life demands that ultimately good and evil be measured and determined with reference to himself. It follows that there are as many gods running around and trying to control things for their own advantage as there are people.

Take the story of the Fall again. The schism it produced is anticipated in the fact that the man and the woman were strategically separated from each other. The woman was alone when she probed behind the words God had spoken and tried to imagine what God was really thinking when He said they should not eat of that tree. The woman was alone when she looked at the tree with her eyes opened, decided that it was good for food, and judged it a delight to the eyes and to be desired to make one wise. And even if the man agreed and joined in the eating, nevertheless each by himself alone had made the decision, in terms of what appeared to be good and desirable over against what seemed less good. Each had done it with reference to himself alone.

The schism became evident very quickly, first of all as a schism from God. For when the LORD God came to them, they hid. Why? Because they judged His coming to be evil for them. And when they came out of hiding, it seemed good to them to distract God with a fashion show and win His awed compliments. But when the LORD continued to press His embarrassing questions, then their loneliness and separation from each other was exposed too. The man blamed the woman. Why? Because by blaming her he could diminish his own guilt. And the woman blamed nature, the serpent. And both of them were blaming God, because the LORD God had made both the woman and the serpent. Thus they fled from evil and pursued good.

We may see already here how the forces of social

disintegration and the forces of cohesion conspire against each other. The fact is that, much as we love our loneliness (for nothing makes a man more lonely than to be like God), we do need the other person. We need other people to notice us and to applaud. We need other people so that we can comfort ourselves in the fact that everybody else does the things we do and that it's only human nature — for then guilt evaporates and we can live with ourselves. We need other people so as to form strategic alliances with them, to add their strength to ours toward attaining the things we consider good.

But in the text of Gen. 3 the LORD God adds two other forces that work for the preservation of society in a world that has become wise, like God. He says to the woman: "Your desire shall be for your husband, and he shall rule over you." That is no mere prediction. It is a divine decree. The woman shall desire marriage and the fulfillment of her sexuality. She is doomed to think that this will be good for her. She is stuck with the romantic illusion that if she gets married she will live happily ever after. It will be her own desire, within the knowledge of good and evil, that binds her to the man. You can see how coldly realistic the LORD is. He does not expect her to *love* that man. Indeed, she cannot. Therefore she must at least *desire* him. Desire becomes the substitute for love. I imagine it would be appropriate to reverse this too, for the man likewise imagines he loves the girl, when he really only wants her.

Yet in the text the role of the man is presented differently. The woman, trapped by her own judgment of good and evil into desiring the man and marriage as good, finds that she has by no means escaped the evil. There is the pain of bearing children and living with them. But the husband himself becomes a pain. "He shall rule over you." Here is another force that makes society cohere in a world

42

in which every man wants to be god. The man shall dominate the woman the way he dominates the plants in the
garden, the way he dominates the beasts and the cattle.
The woman created from his side will now be under him.
Of course the man will find in the process that even marriage cannot relieve the loneliness of one who has become
like god, knowing good and evil.

In any case, the LORD's decree means that in a world
that knows good and evil the strong will dominate the weak,
the people with money and influence will get their way and
those without it will get the leavings. Power counts! That
is an essential principle of fallen society. Be strong, get
educated, get ahead; otherwise you will belong to the domi-
nated and crushed weak of the land. It is good to be the one
who dominates; it is bad to be ruled over, kicked and
bossed around by the strong. So says the knowledge of good
and evil. Climb, climb, climb! And everybody believes it,
even Jesus' disciples. (Matt. 18:1; 20:20-22)

So the man and the woman leave the garden together.
They remain a society of sorts. They agree that it is evil
to expose themselves to God's flaming sword, to let God
kill them by it. Thus their self-protective love of life keeps
them from the tree of life and becomes their death.

But the schism of society is dramatized above all by
the story of their two sons (Gen. 4). Cain knows good and
evil. He knows what is good for him and what is bad for
him. It is intolerable that Abel's sacrifice should be accepted
and his not, that Abel should have a divine approval Cain
does not enjoy. So it is good that Abel should be dead, good
for Cain at least. Since Cain is like God, no other judgment
counts than his own, not even the warning word of God.
This is cacophonous worship—the noise of bitterness and
anger, the deadly blow, the voice of the brother's blood
crying to the LORD from the ground, the voice of Cain

asking, "Am I my brother's keeper?" Add to this the whining complaint, "My punishment is greater than I can bear," and the sound of a city being built, and the sound of musical instruments invented by man and complimenting his mastery over the world, and the sound of Lamech waving a newly invented sword and boasting of his security against attack and his power to dominate other people with it! These sounds all belong to worship, but they are worship within the knowledge of good and evil—man's worship of the gods he creates, of the good he pursues, and of the devices that help him escape the evil he fears. All these sounds prefigure the rupture of society, the hatred and the loneliness of man against man, man no longer able to love his brother, man interested in other people only in terms of the question of advantage or disadvantage, good or evil.

Over against the strain of a society both united and divided by the knowledge of good and evil stands the fellowship of the saints, the society of the family of God, the recovery of humanity as it once was in God's climactic creation. There are three places in which the vision of that humanity comes through to us—first, the creation story; second, the election of Israel; and third, the church.

First, the vision of humanity in the creation. The hint of human society is found in Gen. 1:26-28, where God determines to create man in His own image and give him dominion over all creation, and then creates "them," male and female. The language that started to speak of man in the singular switches suddenly to the plural. "Man" means "man and woman," and to male and female together dominion is given. There is not a ghost of an idea here of domination of one by the other. They are seen as one, and even their children are taken up into the unity of "man" subduing the earth.

But it is in Gen. 2 that this theme is carried through

most consciously and explicitly. As the story begins, the ground is barren. There are no plants, for two reasons. Natural plant life depends on rainfall, and there is none. And the plant life that grows by irrigation cannot occur, because there is no man to do the irrigating. (Since rivers are mentioned but not rain, some such watering seems to be implied.) Now the LORD God takes action. First He forms man from the ground and breathes His own breath into him, and the man lives. Then the LORD plants a garden, puts the man into it, and makes all the trees grow. Man is assigned the task of tilling the ground and keeping the garden.

Then the LORD talks to man about his status, about his authority over the trees and their fruit, and about the one limitation that defines man as creature and the LORD as God. He is over the plants but under God. Thus the man knows God, and by knowing God understands himself. The LORD is the sole source of man's life. Therefore man is to entrust his God with the knowledge of good and evil.

But now the LORD God observes that "it is not good that the man should be alone" and determines to make for him a helper who will stand by him and relieve his loneliness. It is not enough that the man has control of the plants to do with them what he wishes and that he enjoys their fruit. It is not enough that man has the privilege of engaging in theological conversation with God Himself. He is still lonely! So the LORD forms every beast and every bird from the ground and brings them to the man. The man names them, but that only shows that they are under him, even as the plants are. They cannot relieve his loneliness.

Finally the LORD puts the man to sleep. Adam has been very busy with plants and animals, but in this instance he is not busy at all. He does nothing. The LORD God does it all, with no consciousness or cooperation on the man's

45

part whatsoever. Even the judgment that the man is lonely is presented as God's insight alone. The man is not even aware of his own need. Now the LORD forms the woman from the man's rib and brings her to the man. There is immediate recognition. No explanations are required. She is woman, made from himself. They are two, and yet they are one flesh. They stand naked before God. There is nothing to hide, no barrier at all between God and man or between the man and his wife.

That is the perfect society. The intention is that all society that proceeds from that man and woman — the society of parents and children, brothers and sisters, and all degrees of uncles, aunts, and cousins, the whole of the human family — shall forever stand before God and side by side with one another, without plotting or deception, without superiority or inferiority, with nothing hidden or covered, therefore naked and not ashamed. This answers to the judgment of God that the creation is "very good," as in Gen. 1.

I should like to add a comment about this immediacy of recognition between the man and the woman. Some time ago my sons invested in an aquarium. One day I bought two black-lace angelfish to add to their collection. As I watched the fish swimming out of their plastic bag into the tank, it struck me as very remarkable that they remained together, swimming in formation. And then I noticed that a silver angelfish already in the tank swam up to the two black-lace angelfish and joined their formation. And I wondered, "How do they know each other?" How does an angelfish, without consulting a mirror in order to see what he himself looks like, know that he is an angelfish and not a tetra or a guppie or a variata or any of the others? And how did the man know the woman, that she was not an animal but the helper fit for him, corresponding to himself? He just knew, and he knew without mirrors, without analysis, without looking at himself first. That first recognition of the woman utterly transcended any knowledge of good and evil, any knowledge as rational process.

I would infer from this that the awareness one person has of the humanness of another person does not have to depend on a process of intellectual inference. As a matter of fact, intellectual inference can thwart personal recognition, for when man's intellect is absorbed in the questions of good and evil, advantage and disadvantage, he passes his fellows by without seeing them. If he sees them, he only asks how useful they may be to him. He no longer knows them with the immediacy of the recognition that was Adam's when he first saw the woman and welcomed her and knew that she was his own fulfillment, bone of his bone and flesh of his flesh. The clothes we wear are the product of our knowing good and evil. They are designed to cover shame and make a good impression on other people. But they stand in the way of the immediacy of knowledge that was God's gift to the man and the woman originally, the immediacy that lay at the very foundation of their holy society; their oneness even while they were two persons.

Second, the vision of humanity in the election of Israel. The story of God's election of Israel as His people has as an underlying motif the re-creation of His kind of society in a ruptured world. In the background of Abraham's call stands the story of Babel (Gen. 11). The men who gathered to build the tower were a society, to be sure, but a society governed by the knowledge of good and evil. It was to their common advantage to stick together, to make a name for themselves by building a tower with its top in the heavens so that any man who stood there would be god. No knowledge of God is in evidence here, only the pursuit of advantage. Therefore the LORD intervenes to thwart such arrogance. Never shall man succeed in his strategy to achieve good for himself and escape the evil. The builders are scattered. From now on the LORD controls evil by setting man against man, nation against nation, language against language, so that one man's good is another man's evil. This is a vivid description of reality. The very strivings of men against one another are the means by which the LORD shatters the notion that any man is god or even that human society as such may achieve or boast of its deity.

From within that divided and frustrated society the LORD calls one man, Abraham (Gen. 12). He promises to make of him a great nation, to give a land to him and his descendants, and to infect the nations with his blessing. The blessing of Abraham and his power to be the father of a nation rest solely in the word of God, in the divine promise. But to live by the word and promise of God means to give up the knowledge of good and evil. The story of Abraham's great test illustrates this (Gen. 22). If Abraham had known good and evil, he would have judged the command to sacrifice his son Isaac altogether evil and would have found every way possible to evade it, though at the same time pretending to serve God. But Abraham rested in the word of God alone. He did not try to imagine what God might have in mind, as Eve had done. That was his obedience, a quality of obedience to which the son Isaac also surrendered himself. This is what the LORD was after in the people He raised from Abraham's seed. For by such uncalculating trust a very special society will exist, a people bound together by the Word of God and not by their lust for advantage and fear of loss. The story of the schism between Jacob and Esau and then between Joseph and his brothers shows how God's intention was frustrated in practice as Abraham's offspring fell back into the knowledge of good and evil.

48

Then comes the history of the Exodus. It is significant that the very telling of it assumes a kind of corporate unity here. The people of Israel are not a collection of individuals but a single "person," a body. When the LORD says, "I will take you for My people, and I will be your God" (Ex. 6:7), that word binds them both to Himself and to each other. Again, the LORD says to Pharaoh through Moses: "Israel is My firstborn son . . . let My son go that he may serve Me" (Ex. 4:22-23). The sonship is corporate. The people as such are God's son, and He is their Father. They are a very special society, a holy family, bound together to one another by the presence and action of their God. In intervening for them, the LORD remembers the promises He made to their fathers, Abraham, Isaac, and Jacob. Their corporate life as a people goes back to the patriarchs, and it extends in the future to the land of Canaan and its blessings. The passing of generations does not in any way disrupt the continuing life of this people, for every individual knows himself to belong to the whole past and the whole future of that society created by God when He revealed Himself and took them as His own.

It is very remarkable that only sin breaks this picture of unity. Moses reproves two brethren when they are fighting each other in Egypt, and as a consequence he has to flee (Ex. 2:11-15). But his heart remains with his people and their hope. Many of the people, a whole generation of them, fall in the wilderness. But this does not detract from the movement of the corporate history of Israel as God's son, cared for by his Father and given the inheritance of the land.

Much of Israel's law, therefore, emphasizes the solidarity of Israel as brethren bound to one another. They did not create the relationship. They did not choose either God or each other. It is all given, by God's word and creation. They can only receive it, rejoice in it, and express it in their actions toward God and one another.

So their law says: "Love your neighbor as yourself" (Lev. 19:18). What a powerful sentence! For a man's knowing good and evil implies exactly that he loves himself. But God's command is that every man among His people evict himself from the center of decision and put his neighbor there. A man is to ask not what is good or evil for himself, but for the neighbor. He is to act for the neighbor regardless of consequences to himself. But that is possible only for the man who knows that the LORD is his God, the man whose life rests so totally in God's care that he does not have to fear evil or pursue good for himself.

Thus Israel's law sets the knowledge of God against the knowledge of good and evil. On that basis it molds God's kind of society. There are many specific suggestions; for example, generosity to the poor in the laws concerning gleaning (Lev. 19:9-10), hospitality toward the stranger who is *not* a member of God's people (Lev. 19:34) concern for widows and orphans (Deut. 24:19-21). In this last case the problem is not simply that the widow and orphan are economically disadvantaged and impoverished. They are lonely! And love means taking them up into a family again and overcoming the loneliness by incorporating them into society (Deut. 16:11). Nobody is left alone! Israel is a society, God's holy nation, a very special people whom God possesses.

Therefore they need not fear. The future is God's and full of promise. It is a corporate future, which transcends and yet binds into one all the generations. Because the future will come, as the land itself did, in the LORD's own time and way and by His gift, the ultimate good is guaranteed in the face of any and every present experience or threat of evil. That is why Israel is free of the aggressive compulsions of conquest that turn other nations around her into predatory beasts. That is why the prophets can urge kings to yield to the predatory enemy without fighting back or resorting to alliances, and to endure whatever the consequences may be in the way of loss and suffering, pain and darkness (Is. 7: 1-9). For God's people suffer together, and they have one another to support and strengthen. Thus they manifest their holiness and the holiness of their God. Then the nations will begin to take notice, and they will ask about the blessing of Abraham—above all when they discover that the good they pursued turns to evil and the evil they dreaded for themselves but inflicted on Israel is turned to Israel's good (Is. 60:1-14). Then the holy infection of Israel will infect the nations, the whole of the humanity to which Israel also belongs.

The history, of course, is far more the story of failure than of success. The vision of what ought to be is clear to the prophets, but how to perform it turns out to be beyond the capacity of fleshly Israel. The glitter of good captures the eye of God's people too, and they grasp for it as lustfully as their neighbors do. The dread of suffering and evil and injustice repels them, so that they resist it bitterly. Like any pagan nation they invoke the name of their God on their enterprise of securing the good and avoiding the evil (Jer. 7:3-11); and when God turns against them, they hate Him or fall into despair and think He is dead.

So the great society is divided. There is the terrible division of the northern kingdom from the southern in the days of Rehoboam (1 Kings 12). There is the social chasm between the nobility, landowners, kings, and the poor and suffering (Amos 4:1-3; 6:1-7). The latter can be trampled the more because they have so little to contribute to the enterprises of national glory and salvation that seem so overwhelmingly important to the kings and princes. Hence the kings who are supposed to be God's shepherds become predatory beasts instead, devouring their own flock, eating the fat and clothing themselves with the wool of the poor instead of caring for and feeding the sheep and seeking the lost and strayed (Ezek. 34). As a result, Israel is destroyed, Jerusalem falls, the temple is burned, the people who survive are deported.

Then the Lord comes to them even in a strange land and brings a tiny remnant home. But they still love the knowledge of good and evil more than God. They still will not be God's kind of society. And when Jesus comes to be to the full what Israel, as the son of God (Ex. 4:22), should have been and was not, they turn against Him and put Him to death.

We are back again at that decisive moment of Jesus. It is a very strange piece of history, when you examine it from the perspective of the theme of *fellowship,* the relation of man to his brother. For Jesus stood thoroughly within His people. He was one of them. He knew their God as His God, their heavenly Father as His heavenly Father, their promises as His promises, their hope as His hope, their calling as His calling. Their Bible was also His Bible, their history His history, their worship His worship. We must learn better than we have the importance of starting with this, for here lies the continuity between Old Testament Israel and ourselves as the people of God.

When Jesus talks to Israel, He is addressing His brethren and speaking their language. There is nothing obscure in what He says. If they come to hate Him, they do so for reasons that are very clear to them. What Jesus is after is a people bound to their heavenly Father so that they can be bound to one another. That is exactly what God had wanted all along. It is a terrible paradox that the people of God, instead of sensing their unity with Jesus, find Him to be a disruptive force in the society they have created. They defend themselves by isolating and rejecting Him.

Let us trace this briefly. Start with Jesus in the temple, saying to His parents in great simplicity, "Didn't you know that I must be about My Father's business?" (Luke 2:49). There is nothing inherently difficult about that saying. Jesus and His parents belonged to Israel, and God had called Israel "My son" way back in the Exodus history. "Israel is My firstborn son . . . let My son go that he may serve Me" (Ex. 4:22-23). That sentence qualifies Jesus, as a son of Israel, to call God "My Father." But its implications are equally clear. The son is to *serve* the Father. That is exactly Jesus' point. "I must be about My Father's business." If His parents didn't understand, it was because Judaism in general did not understand. Only when Jesus had *served* to the point of laying down His life as a ransom for many did anyone really understand what the familiar and ancient sentence really meant. But now Jesus goes home and serves His parents. Within His own family in Nazareth He takes His full place in the family of God's people.

Next comes the cry, "Repent, for the kingdom of heaven is at hand" (Matt. 3:1-12). The day of the Lord means both judgment and salvation, however. To the people of God, that is, the righteous, it means salvation. To outsiders and sinners it means destruction, for the Kingdom is to be given to Israel as their inheritance. Yet, as John the Baptist already makes clear, the judgment begins at the house of God. Even the Pharisee must repent, let go all security and advantage of his own past, and wait for the Lord to open the new future on His own terms.

Jesus hears the call of John the Baptist. He commits Himself totally, lets go of His past, is baptized, and stands free and ready to do the will of His heavenly Father (Matt. 3:13-17). The will of His Father now is that He carry the cry of the Kingdom to His home territory, Galilee (Matt. 3:12-17). The Galileans are under suspicion for their mixed blood, and there is some question in the minds of the theologians in Judaea as to what their status in the coming kingdom will be.

Certainly it will be inferior, it is assumed. But Jesus goes to those whose status is doubtful and marginal, and to those who by every view of the Law are to be rejected. He seeks the lost, the excommunicated tax collectors and harlots, who had forfeited all hope of being in on the blessing of the Kingdom. In the name of the mercy of the heavenly Father, perhaps even by Baptism, He takes them in freely and fully. They belong again. The are fully qualified for the Kingdom. He finds the sick and suffering, those who in their very disabled bodies experience the exclusion and disapproval of God and of men, and He takes these people in by healing them. The mercy of God to sinners overflows in Him to the very people over whom Pharisees asserted their religious superiority.

But how shall we now interpret His actions? Two views are possible. One is presented by the Pharisees. For one thing, the cry that the Kingdom is coming is itself both doubtful and dangerous, so the opponents argue. Jesus and John the Baptist have gotten the people all worked up in a zealotic frenzy, so that the violent are ready to take the Kingdom by force (Matt. 11:12) and a disastrous clash with Roman authority is in the making. If the Kingdom were really coming at this moment, God would give some *sign* of it (Matt. 12:38), and not expect theologians to accept the word of a couple of fanatics. Furthermore, Jesus clearly violates the Law. For righteousness is by the Law. The Law defines clearly how God's people are to preserve their holiness and distinctiveness from all others. The Pharisees observe the Sabbath, wash their hands before meals, eat kosher foods, and engage in honorable occupations. But Jesus encourages contempt for the Law by healing on the Sabbath in cases where there is clearly no emergency, by not washing hands before meals, by associating with sinners, and by taking in tax collectors and harlots whom the Law excludes. Thus He is a sinner and a fanatic, and He must be silenced before He completely undermines both the Law and the nation.

The argument is very persuasive. Notice, however, that it operates completely under and by the knowledge of good and evil. Man looks ahead and calculates consequences, and he determines his present actions in such a way as to minimize the evil and maximize the good. But at the heart of this thinking lies the advantage of the Pharisee himself. He knows why he keeps the Law, as Jesus points out, namely for the reward or profit he hopes to get from it. And the real reason he rejects the message of the Kingdom is that he cannot trust any word of God at all without subjecting it first to his own critical judgment and deciding the issue on the basis of consequences. "An evil and adulterous [that is, idolatrous] generation seeks for a sign." (Matt. 16:4)

Jesus' own actions make sense only when you see Him transcending the knowledge of good and evil by simple and total faith in His Father. He does not fear evil or pursue good for Himself. He only does the will of His Father. He loves the Lord His God with all His heart, soul, strength, and mind, and His neighbor as Himself. The future is the Father's business, including the whole meaning and form of the coming kingdom. His business is to find the lost, the poor, the suffering, the despairing, to draw them into the society of Israel by drawing them into fellowship with Himself (Luke 19:10). Love that transcends the knowledge of good and evil will endure evil and threat without resistance (Matt. 5:39). Love will give in to cruel and unjust men who enjoy abusing the weak. Men filled with God's kind of love cannot hate the Romans and desire their destruction, just as the LORD could not allow Jonah of old to hate the city of Nineveh and delight in seeing 120,000 little children destroyed out of self-pity and for the encouragement of his own vanity (Jonah 4). That was the kind of case Jesus made. "Go and learn what this means, 'I desire mercy and not sacrifice,' " He said to those who objected. (Matt. 9:13)

It turned out, however, that the very men who seemed to be the righteous in Israel were in the most hopeless state of all, possessed by "seven devils" (Matt. 12:45). Jesus set Himself against all the pressures of Pharisee and priest, against all the religious authority in Jerusalem, without regard to consequences. He could not let them go the way they were going. He had to press the issue to its ultimate conclusion. That was the will of His Father, and the Son had nothing to do but to serve the Father. The business of protecting Him or of bringing in the Kingdom, all this Jesus committed to His Father. At Gethsemane He gave up the knowledge of good and evil. He would not be afraid of men or of death (Matt. 26:36-46). His enemies paid Him a remarkable compliment when they acknowledged that He did not "regard the position of men" (Matt. 22:16). That meant He did not know good and evil. He did not judge people by their clothes or prestige or power. He knew only the Father, and His call was to gather the lost among His brethren and bring them back to the Father.

Out of that clash came His death. He claimed to be the Son of God, but in their own way (they were not so bold in their theological language) so did the high priest and the elders. It was impossible for both claims to stand. The Sanhedrin charged Him with blasphemy and thus cast Him out as a sinner worthy of death (Matt. 26:63-66). He died alone, outside Jerusalem, rejected by the very people He loved. When He died even His disciples knew only fear and despair. Life ended for them too. Their hopes were dead. He was isolated and alone. That is why in the ultimate sense only one man has the name "Son of God" which belonged to all Israel, and that is Jesus. And the name "Son of Man," used in Dan. 7 to picture God's people as receiving the promise, becomes His alone. And the name "the Righteous One," He alone possesses it (Luke 23:47; Acts 3:14; 7:52; Rom.5:

17-19; 1 John 2:1). And He alone received the Kingdom from the Father, when God raised Him from the dead and set Him at His own right hand in the heavenly places, far above every name that is named in heaven and on earth.

That is why the Old Testament came to an end with Jesus' death and resurrection. The righteousness the Pharisee had claimed under the Law could not count any more now as a means of identifying him as God's son and heir. After the Resurrection, how could those who had pronounced Jesus a sinner still boast before God of their circumcision, their Sabbath, their kosher meats, their fringed garments? How could they boast of Jerusalem and the temple? All this belonged to the old garment, now beyond patching. It constituted the old wineskins, but the old wine was exhausted and the new wine could not go into those bottles (Matt. 9: 16-17). How could the city and temple that conspired to crucify the only Son of God still be God's dwelling place? "Your house is forsaken and desolate" (Matt. 23:38). God has moved out. So the temple went down in Jesus' death. The new temple is Jesus' body (John 2:18-22). The Lord seeks people who will worship Him neither in Jerusalem nor on the Samaritan mountain Gerizim, but in spirit and in truth. (John 4:21-24)

That is why Jesus must also remain at the center — not merely a symbol but the concrete Person in whose very flesh God was incarnate and spoke to men. When the Kingdom would have destroyed the world and left only Jesus, God granted the world a reprieve and an eternal hope by making His whole wrath, as well as the wrath of devils and of ungodly men, fall in one terrible moment on His Son. So now all the old names of Israel have passed through Christ and become ours. It is Baptism, not circumcision or any other law, that identifies us with Him as sons of God, heirs of the promises of His coming, saints, God's holy people and family (Gal. 3:23 — 4:7). That is why Jesus' death also broke down all the old barriers between Jew and Gentile, so that the cry of the Kingdom could go to the nations and participation in the family of God be offered freely to a lost world. That is why the Jew must wear the wedding garment of the blood of Christ (Matt. 22:11-14). That is why the great name of God we hallow, and which contains the whole of our history for us, is no longer "Yahweh" as in the Old Testament but "the name of the Father and of the Son and of the Holy Ghost."

Third, the vision of humanity in the church. The event of the New Testament brought another terrible schism into God's people, and the writings of the New Testament feel the tragedy very strongly. It was the separation of the church from Judaism. That the healing of that schism may still come was St. Paul's great hope and prayer (Rom. 9−11). Meanwhile, however, the church is the fellowship of the saints, the family of the heavenly Father, the body of Christ. The love of Christ breaks through to us when we are outsiders and under wrath, gathers us into the flock, and names us God's eternal elect people, by grace alone, through faith in the Word and promise that gives us so high an identity.

But that identity and call has transforming power. The old Adam with his knowledge of good and evil dies, and the new man that comes forth daily in repentance and in the remembrance of our baptism is the little child, resting in the bosom of the Father, ignorant of good and evil. "If anyone is in Christ, he is a new creation; the old has passed away, behold, the new has come" (2 Cor. 5:17). Now we don't owe anything to the flesh, this human nature in which we were naturally born. We don't owe anything to any man, except to love one another, as Christ has loved us, to the glory of God (Rom. 13:8-10). The new man is in the image of God, created "in true righteousness and holiness" (Eph. 4:24). We live not to ourselves anymore, but to Him who died for us and rose again. (2 Cor. 5:15)

This means that we know God. We do not rebel against being creatures. Our creaturely limitation is the starting point from which we work, and as long as it is the starting point and not a restraint against which we rebel, we are free. But once we are not fighting our creatureliness, we are no longer trying to be god either. Our eyes are not turned on ourselves but on God and on His will.

It is really a remarkable thing. All the old battles, the old fears, the old lusts fall away. They are so silly and meaningless. Here I thought I had to prove myself and make something of my life. I don't have to do any such thing! My God is creating my life, and He knows where He is taking me even if I don't.

I was so concerned about making a proper impression or defending myself against accusations. I hated to be wrong or to appear stupid and ignorant. How silly it all was! To imagine that I could know good and evil!

I thought I was out in the middle of nowhere, with no past and no future, all alone even when surrounded by people, so directionless that I even hated life. How foolish and blind I was until the Word of God found me in my darkness, freed me from the burden of concern for defining past and future, and called me to the glory of the life that is mine now!

I was afraid, afraid of being guilty and being discovered so, afraid of a thousand potential catastrophes, afraid of being a loser, so afraid that I could not even enjoy pleasure for fear it would end. How ungodly were my fears and how free I am in the arms of my God and my Christ, who is my Wisdom, Righteousness, Sanctification, and Redemption! (1 Cor. 1:30)

So I am free of the knowledge of good and evil. And now I know who I am. I discover my individuality, all the uniqueness of God's gifts, so that I don't have to feel either superior or inferior, for I am what God wants me to be and also where He wants me, and that is riches enough.

But I discover also my individuality in community. I belong to humanity. The whole organic history of man enfolds me. I have a partnership in the human race, in all that came before and bore me, in all that will come after me. But I know that humanity as such is the old Adam, sick and in death, trying so desperately to know good and evil. I can understand and sympathize, for I am so much of that nature myself. But I belong above all to the new humanity, to the body of Christ, the new Adam, the infection of life in the old, to the living temple where the Spirit dwells and in which God lives and works and manifests Himself to men. I belong to the history of Abraham and of Israel, of Christ and of the church, to all the saints who came before me and will come after me. I am an individual, yet I am not just an individual, for I belong to Christ and to Christ's holy people. I shall be as small or as big as the Lord wants me to be!

Here is the freedom that restores people to one another, that breaks the terrible loneliness. We can stop calculating, and start seeing one another. Not by logical analysis but by the simplicity of personal contact we know our common humanity. It starts in the church, for the church is the holy community, distinct from the world, filled with the life and power of the Spirit of God. The ambiguity of the conflict between our sinnerhood and sainthood continues, of course. Yet the Spirit of God enables us to look at the world and life and each other in freedom from the knowledge of good and evil. That is the end of all fear and self-consciousness, of all shame and impression-making.

So look at your brother and discover that he is a person like yourself! And as you know yourself, so you will know him. Be a strength to him in his weakness, and let him be a strength to you. Rejoice when he rejoices, and weep when he weeps! Never pass him by, as though you could ever rise above him and so look down on him. You do him no service of love when he must look up at you, when he is dragging behind you, or even when you artificially or by some fleshly measure of reality are below him. Do not fear him or stand in awe of him. Know him and let him know you, in the freedom and laughter of the sons of God who, in Christ, can be foolish and sinful without fear.

The church is the community of people who are united in one Lord Jesus, enjoy one common freedom, and can therefore create the community the world so much needs. When we gather in worship together, it is as though the body of Christ is inhaling and drawing all the resources of the Spirit (Breath) of God into itself as a common possession. When we leave our worship it is as though the body of Christ exhales, breathing us into our separate communities and associations renewed in the life of God and able in all good cheer to infect the world around us with our freedom. Nothing can shatter that unity in Christ.

We have a variety of gifts, but they are all gifts of God and the Spirit (1 Cor. 12:4-31; Eph. 4:1-16). In the eyes of the world outside, the variation in gifts would set some higher than others, some on the top and some on the bottom, for the eyes of the world see by the knowledge of good and evil. But we see with the vision of our God. We are not alike; that is why we can be a body. Yet we are all alike. For we are all sinners, doomed to the dust of death. We have all tasted the tree of the knowledge of good and evil, know its terrible attraction and its even more terrible curse. We are all redeemed to God by mercy alone, by the initiative of the Father alone, through the one blood of Jesus Christ. We all share one Baptism. We all know the glory of the Gospel, which makes it impossible any longer to respect persons, to look at the degrees of men or the color of men or the status of men. By the knowledge of good and evil we would judge and evaluate one another. But in freedom from that knowledge we can truly know and love one another, as the Father has loved us in Jesus Christ our Lord.

So the works of love follow. The sons of God have no will except God's will, no purpose except to hear the word of the Lord, "Follow Me." They don't ask whether it is dark or dangerous, or whether they will lose too much. They follow and obey, for that is their life. Their hearts are full of the "Hallelujah!" of perpetual thanksgiving, and every drop of water they drink is occasion for a song of praise. They know how to give freely, holding nothing back by calculation, for they know that the Father gives more abundantly than they can dream of, and He will take care of their tomorrow. Because they receive for nothing, they also give for nothing (Matt. 10:8) and will not be dismayed by lack of appreciation or recognition or glory. They can also forgive sins, bear insults, and go the second mile, for the measure of their status is not the recognition they receive from men, but the Word of God. No contempt or injustice of men can take that treasure of promise from them. Thus the bond of fellowship grows as they experience the power of love for one another in the community of the saints. They watch for one another so that no one will be lost, no tear be shed alone, no experience of blessing lack a shared hallelujah, no hunger go unfed.

That is what goes on in the fellowship of the redeemed, the Christian parish. The love that shines there spills over into the world. And the world, seeing it happen there and spilling over, takes note of its peculiar spirit of freedom, joy, and confidence. And when it does, a world lost in its knowledge of good and evil finds itself touched by the holy infection of the communion of saints.

3

In the Relativism of Men —
The Eternal Truth (Education)

Everybody recognizes today that the business of education has become enormously complex and faces overwhelming difficulties. One problem is simply the explosion of knowledge and the consequent fragmentization of disciplines. No man today dares to say what Francis Bacon said almost four centuries ago: "I have taken all knowledge to be my province." The fields of knowledge have multiplied vastly. Philosophy and science were once interchangeable terms. Now they are separate disciplines. Science has divided and subdivided itself again and again, so that a man who wants to work at the frontiers of research must be the narrowest of specialists. Most of the social sciences have come into existence only in the last century or so. And in the older social sciences, for example, history, we are forced by the very contraction of our world and the breakdown of the older isolations to get to know the history of continents and people who never much concerned us before, to know their mind and religion and literature as well as our own.

It is a frightening business today, the business of trying to be an educated man. It is frightening even in theology. For there is Biblical theology with all its new techniques and subject areas, and there are systematic theology and historical theology and all the aspects that are supposedly covered in the catchall called practical theology.

There are ecumenism and missions and healing. There are the pioneer or frontier theologians who try to relate theology to psychology and sociology and various philosophies and anthropologies. There are books and slogans and names galore that educated theologians are supposed to know how to toss around. And the printing presses keep rolling and producing periodicals. So you feel terribly inferior when somebody says, "Have you read—?" and you say no. And a dozen other books are mentioned, and you keep saying no. What is a theologian supposed to be, anyhow? A computer? But theology is only one tiny branch of the whole of learning. Every discipline, every science is faced with a parallel torment, the impossibility of keeping up with the burst of facts and ideas or of knowing what is important enough to deserve attention when everything shouts for attention.

Here then is the problem of education today, not only Christian education but education generally. What is an educated man? What should he know? How much should he know? The demand is great, the pressures are heavy. Grade schools have to cover ground once covered in high schools, because high schools have to cover ground once reserved for colleges, because universities have to cover ground once reserved for graduate schools and research institutions. Once it was enough to know how to read. Now you have to be able to read 1,000 words a minute or, if possible, 2,000. Thus the cleavage between those who can do the work and those who cannot becomes greater and greater. And whereas we once spoke of the poor kid who didn't have what it took to go to high school, we now pity the poor kid who can't get accepted into graduate school. And when a man gets his doctorate and has written a thesis on some obscure theme that makes him for the moment the world's greatest expert on that particular subject, we still find ourselves asking what we mean when we call him an educated man.

The problem of education today goes beyond the fragmentation and proliferation of knowledge. There is also the nagging question of the relativism of the whole human situation and the reluctance to speak of "truth." Relativism is an inevitable by-product of an age of science. For the scientific mind is insatiably curious and skeptical—curious to understand phenomena in relation to each other, skeptical of any prior understanding that fails to encompass and do full justice to all the facts. Scientific inquiry presupposes the freedom to doubt any accepted way of seeing things and to look more closely to see whether it is really so. Everything has to be proved or be forced to prove itself. There is no absolute truth, no universal principle to which there may not be some exception. This posture of initial curiosity coupled with skepticism has been tremendously fruitful, of course. It has led to the most intensive examination of evidences, to marvelous experimentation and instrumentation, to the overthrow of a thousand traditional views. Methodological skepticism has led, in short, to that burst of science and technology which is the marvel of our age.

But the posture of skepticism also places a premium on the judgment to be rendered in every situation by every individual. Not only is there no absolute truth in itself; even proximate truth achieves consensus only as it is able to persuade individuals who encounter it. To "think" means to accept nothing on sheer authority but to judge and be responsible for that "truth" by which one will live. Every individual must be ready to answer for his own responses and accept the consequences. No individual has the right or authority simply to force his way of thinking on another, for that would be to violate the integrity of the other.

One effect of this relativism is that men call into question the entire social order and subject the whole system of society to the judgment of every member. The relativism of modern thought engenders suspicion of authority. We encourage one another not to believe, not to trust public officials or police or courts or laws or newspapers or parents or God or even the Ten Commandments. Everything is up for constant reevaluation and decision by every individual. Nobody can provide for anybody else the ground on which to stand. Every individual must find that ground for himself.

This is the prevailing philosophy, a by-product, I think, of scientific skepticism. This is the outlook on life being engendered not only in American public schools but by and in the whole social system. It leaves every individual free and responsible—but also profoundly lonely. For there is no more terrible loneliness for a man than to have to be like God, making his lonely decision as to what is good and what is evil.

Relativism sounds like a great and noble principle, but it has a way of driving our brightest youth to distraction. They can take nothing for granted, not even their own existence. They feel compelled to answer the ultimate questions: Who am I? What is life all about? What is valuable? What am I doing here? They are burdened with the terrible necessity of being wise, of making decisions they cannot make, of answering questions they cannot answer. And parents, caught up in the same world of relativism, retreat from their authority as parents, doubting both their right and their qualifications to exercise judgment over and for their children, unable themselves to answer the questions. It should be no surprise, then, that our world erupts in social chaos, for it must erupt. It may sound very noble to make every man a god, yet the consequence has to be that every man is an idol.

Let us carry the problem one step further. The purpose of education is to make men wise, it is said. Obviously the purpose cannot be to make everybody know everything, since that is quite impossible. When it comes to "knowing things," the most that education can do is equip a person to find out what he may want to know. Thus we teach our children to read or to think, though even that is quite a problem. Certainly we want to teach them what they need to know to hold a job and be productive in society. But to make a living and be able to look up things in an encyclopedia hardly seems worthy as the goal of education.

Therefore we say that we educate in order to make young people *wise*. But what is wisdom? In part, to be wise is to be a skeptic, as when one youth tells another to "wise up!" But we mean more than that. Wisdom as a goal of education, I suggest, can hardly be better defined than the way the serpent defined it in Gen. 3. To be wise means to be like God, knowing good and evil. To know good and evil means to look into the potential consequences of a present action, take all factors into account and then act in the way that will result in the most good and the least evil. A refined knowledge of good and evil is one that reckons with the fact that a little evil or suffering now may be a bargain in the long run and that one's private good or evil is inseparable from the good or evil to be experienced by society. In some cases it is not merely one's own immediate society that needs to be considered, but society as large as the world.

Take one practical example of how such wisdom operates. Fifteen years ago President Eisenhower made the decision after the partition of Vietnam that a token American presence should fill the vacuum left by the French defeat and withdrawal. Such action, regrettable as it might be in itself, would obviate far greater evils later, namely a predatory Communist expansion that would fatten itself by devouring the whole of southeast Asia. That was strictly knowledge-of-good-and-evil wisdom, in the best tradition of the contemporary American ideal. Those who have opposed it are

67

also trying to be wise, to know good and evil, to take the action now that will minimize the future evil and maximize the good. Some of them are very confident that they know what should be done, even arrogant in their confidence. But the fact is that nobody really knows, because nobody can anticipate all future possibilities.

We know good and evil at best to a very limited extent. We may be wise enough to live within a budget or to run out and close the back gate so the baby won't run into the street or to get a tetanus shot when we have stepped on a nail. But we often show ourselves not wise enough even for such simple things. We may not be wise enough to give up smoking in the face of many threatening evidences — though on the other hand, if life today would be unbearable without that smoke, who can say what the course of wisdom really is? And if you don't know what life is all about anyhow, why prolong it? And if there is a chance that cancer might not hit you anyhow, but only the other fellow, why not take the chance? It is a complicated business, knowing good and evil. Even when we can know, it is a question whether the present convenience may not outweigh the intangible future good.

So who is to say what wisdom really is? Every individual must decide. And we are back at the relativism of it all. There are no final answers. Maybe Pilate's answer had a lot of practical justification: "What is truth?" (John 18:38). To Pilate the answer is immaterial. What matters is not what is true but who's got the power to make his will stick. That is relativism at its best — or worst — depending on whether you think relativism is good or evil. It is your decision, and mine, and everybody's.

Thus our world, with all its education and science and wisdom and skepticism and responsibility and individuality, finds itself on a dark sea of uncertainty. There may be optimism here and there about the future of mankind, and just enough hints of potential glory, like putting a man on the moon, to feed the optimism. But there is great reason for fear and pessimism too. Things may be going fairly well for us in our pleasant suburb, but we do not know whether our situation is booby-trapped with some secret dynamite. If we were capable of the superstition of the ancient Canaanites, we would be running to our astrologers and magicians and necromancers and augurers and wizards. But since we cannot run to these, we run to our politicians and columnists and commentators (you notice I did not say theologians), hoping that they will have the answers we lack and fill us in on the knowledge of good and evil that is beyond us. Man, caught in the necessity of knowing good and evil, yet finding himself unable to know, passes the problem on to his children. Maybe the next generation will do better than this one. In any case wisdom, for all the freedom it promises, turns out to be quite a prison, a great burden.

Against all this, Christian education presents, or has the opportunity to present, a rather remarkable contrast. There must be a contrast, otherwise the concept of holiness and the power to be a salt and a light are voided. But the contrast must also be understood. It is all too easy for the church to substitute an authoritarian dogmatism for the Gospel or to claim eternal truth for elements of its tradition that do not belong to the Gospel at all. Thus it becomes necessary to define both what the eternal truth is and how it is transmitted in the process we call Christian education. Ultimately the content and the means of transmitting it are inseparable.

It is clear enough in many Biblical texts that the people of God must repudiate the relativism of the modern world and inject a note of wholesome skepticism against the supposition of scientific thought that man must always be the skeptic. Ps. 90 begins: "LORD, Thou hast been our dwelling place in all generations." That suggests that an unfailing truth concerning God as the total source of Israel's life and security has been passed down from generation to generation and will not be repudiated by the skepticism of men. Is. 40:6-8 states that "all flesh is grass" but that "the Word of our God will stand forever." In spite of great progress in medicine, the verdict that all flesh is grass still stands. The Word of our God with its promises also stands. Neither death nor the Word of God will submit to relativism. Again, the LORD declares: "I am the First and the Last, and besides Me there is no god" (Is. 44:6). There is no room for relativism in that sentence. Mary in the Magnificat sings: "His mercy is on those who fear Him from generation to generation" (Luke 1:50). And Jesus declares: "Heaven and earth will pass away, but My words will not pass away." (Luke 21:33)

That Word of God and of Christ is a promise that overthrows and condemns all the wisdom of man, all the pride and responsibility, all the relativism of truth. It is a remarkably simple Word, easily heard and learned. But it will not submit to human skepticism, to demands for proof. For when skepticism attacks the Word of God, the Word of God turns on the skeptic and accuses him of still trying to be god. That is one privilege the Word of God cannot concede or tolerate.

At its very simplest the Word of God is the Word He spoke upon us in our baptism. When we were baptized it was as though God the Father spoke from heaven upon us the Word Jesus heard at His baptism: "This is My beloved son, with whom I am well pleased." That Word is always from heaven, from God Himself, even if we do not hear it as a booming mysterious voice from the clouds. It may come through the earthy touch of common ordinary water. But it is nevertheless the eternal, unfailing affirmation of God, the indelible Word, which no accusation of devils or men can erase or silence, which stands for eternity, and which condemns as liars all men who try to resist or contradict it.

It is a very old Word. By it God took Israel in Egypt as His people against all the glory and might of Pharaoh: "Thus says the LORD, 'Israel is My firstborn son . . . let My son go that he may serve Me' " (Ex. 4:22-23). All the other terminology by which God identified this people as His own simply repeats the same fundamental idea. He calls them "My people," "My vineyard," "My sheep," "My wife." They are that, however, not by right of what they have done but by the Word alone. They are God's son because God said so, and when God says a thing, it is so.

Thus the covenant Word was Israel's security against all threat and evil, and the source of all their blessing and good. That Word upheld them even when they sinned, for God's Word is stubborn in its determination, and God, however He chastized them, would not let them go. If Israel will not hallow God's name, God will take action and do it Himself—but that name is going to be hallowed on earth! *That's* how stubborn God is. (Read Ezek. 36; Is. 59; 63.)

That Word had its fulfillment in Jesus and in Him alone, as we have seen. And through Jesus' atoning death and resurrection that Word has passed to us and made us the people of God. We are authorized and commanded to pray, "*Our Father* who art in heaven, hallowed be Thy name." "For in Christ Jesus you are all sons of God, through faith. For as many of you as were baptized into Christ have put on Christ. . . . You are all one in Christ Jesus. And if you are Christ's then you are Abraham's offspring, heirs according to promise." (Gal. 3:26-29)

The Word of God declares us to be God's sons through Christ and enables us to trace our genealogies back to Abraham in continuity of identity with the covenant people of old. The Word of God holds us secure under the Father's blessing and promise for our immediate and ultimate tomorrow. That

Word is the eternal truth, which holds firm against all the relativism of the modern world. It is the core of knowledge around which all fragmentary scientific knowledge rotates. It is the wisdom that defies and overthrows all the wisdom of men. It is the eternal wisdom so simple that children, but only children, can grasp it. This wisdom is the core of Christian education. It makes Christian education a holy infection in a world full of every kind of knowledge except the knowledge it needs most, the knowledge of God.

"One little word can fell him," Luther sang in defiance of all threat and suffering the devil hurled against him. That one little word was *baptizatus sum,* "I am baptized." All of Christian theology is comprehended in that little word. Who am I? I am a child of God, a member of Christ's holy people. I have a dignity and honor, an eternal worth, that no experience of suffering and no judgment of human contempt can take from me. I am not a nothing out in the middle of nowhere. I am not subject to the judgments of men. I have an identity and a name. I belong to God and to God's family, to the people whom God my Father has made a core of life in a humanity doomed to death. That's who I am, and no evidence of shame or even of my own sin and failure can take that name and treasure away from me.

But *how* am I that? Not by anything I did or deserved. I did not create myself or ask to be born. The life I have in this flesh, every breath and every day of it, every inch of growth from infancy to adulthood (Matt. 6:27), is a continual unfolding of the gifts and care of my heavenly Father. So also my baptismal birth into God's family came to me freely and for nothing, not by my desire but by the will of God. That's what it means to be born. I have an inheritance and a status not by works of righteousness, not by climbing to the stars, not by comparing myself and my potential and achievements with other people, but solely by God's purpose and mercy.

To know my Father is to know my birthright, to recognize that I am what I am by right of birth — both the creative birth of body and life and the redemptive birth of baptism into the sonship and knowledge of God. Thus I rejoice to be *man,* not God; a *creature,* not my own creator. I rejoice to receive what I have and what is continually being given me. I shall not strive frantically for pursuits and ambitions of my own apart from my God and Father.

But how do I *know* that all this is so? I know because God has told me so in my own baptism when He said of me: "This is My beloved son." That baptism of mine encompasses a whole history. It has meaning and power because it is filled with the history of Jesus, who was baptized, who knew His Father, trusted Him, served and obeyed Him even to death, "who was delivered for our offenses and was raised again for our justification" (Rom. 4:25). And Jesus' own baptism and death have meaning because they stand in the context of the whole history of Israel and fulfill it. And Israel's history has meaning because this people was called to be God's own by the Father Almighty, Maker of heaven and earth.

But if I still press the question and demand that God give me some other sign from heaven or prove Himself in some other way, then God laughs at my impudence. For once again I want to be like God. I insist that I must submit God's Word to my own judgment, as though it were mine to decide whether it is reliable and worth believing. Once again I want to live by my knowledge of good and evil. But that is exactly my death! "Therefore," says God, "there is no way that I can allow you to judge My Word. When I speak, you are the creature, and My Word judges you. If you will not hear My verdict of mercy in Baptism, then you will have to hear My verdict in your fear and frustration. That verdict speaks of nothing but wrath and death. There is no way you can know or find Me unless I first know and find you. Nor is there any way for you to receive My Word other than to believe it, throw yourself gladly on My mercy, and join with My saints in their quiet and joyful hallelujah."

But if I ask, "What does this Word of God declaring me to be God's son mean for my future?" it means that my life can no longer be governed by my knowledge of good and evil, for that knowledge I leave entirely to God. The future is full of promise, for even the last enemy, death, is conquered and has no power over me. The mouths of the lions are shut (Dan. 6), the flames of the fiery furnace cannot singe a hair of my head (Dan. 3). All things work out for good to those who love God and share in His eternal purposes (Rom. 8:28). If God is for us, who is against us? (Rom. 8:31). Tomorrow and all its consequences belong to God. He gives us, His children, the bread we need and knows our needs before we ask Him.

Therefore we are free of the knowledge of good and evil. The question cannot be, "Will it hurt?" or, "What profit will I get out of it?" The question is only, "Lord, what do You want me to do?" For life consists in knowing the Father through Christ, following as He leads, and fulfilling His creative purposes.

That is the truth of the Word of God. It stands from generation to generation. There is nothing relative about it. It is neither ancient nor modern. It is eternal, and it carries the power of life now and of resurrection from the dead. In the midst of the relativism of men, that Word and the power of its life is the subject matter of Christian education.

It is obvious, therefore, that Christian education belongs to and can only happen within the society of the people of God. Society as it exists among men within and by the knowledge of good and evil must also educate, as we have seen. As surely as generations come and go and children are born in the flesh, they must be taken up into the society of which they are a part. For all its radical individualism even American secular society must reckon with the concept that humanity is in some sense an organism that encompasses all individuals and transcends all generations. When individuals can find no meaning, or confront the reality of their little achievement, they project the dreams and hopes that have died in them onto their children. Perhaps "mankind" as such will continue the upward march to some great and enduring glory! At least each generation wants to imagine that it has contributed along the way, that it is a step ahead of the last. And so culture and ideas accumulate, and the corporate memory of man by way of education is able to absorb and build on the whole of the human past. Whether the notion of progress upward is real or whether it is merely the illusory hope of a humankind that cannot endure the thought of failure and therefore blinds itself to defeat and sees and remembers only what contributes to its self-flattery and glory—that is very difficult even for secular men to determine.

At any rate, secular education at its best is dedicated to the preservation and progress of human ideas, to the pursuit of good and the escape from evil—not for the advantage of the individual only but for the whole of humankind. That is the vision that must be realized in each generation and yet transcends all generations. And the man who can in some small way tell himself how he has contributed to that upward ascent of the race can thereby enjoy a sense of importance and believe that his life has meaning. To that conception education in its noblest secular sense is dedicated.

As secular education can occur only within the community of men who are wise in the knowledge of good and evil, so Christian education can occur only in the communion of saints, who are wise in the fear of the LORD. Christians belong to the whole of humanity, but they belong to it as a tissue of life in a body of cancer or gangrene destined for death. Christians need to be very clear on the alternative they represent. They know that the knowledge of good and evil has a certain validity and importance, given the world as it is. But they know that the judgment of God still stands: "The day you eat thereof you shall surely *die*." There is no hope that man can really succeed in his climb to the stars by way of the wisdom to which he is so determinedly committed. "Whoever exalts himself shall be abased." That is the inexorable law for every individual and for corporate humanity as well.

Therefore the church transmits to its children, from generation to generation, the knowledge of God. It does this even as it asserts and preserves its holiness, the separateness of its identity, over against the world in which it stands.

We can learn much about the process of the transmission of God's kind of life by examining the way education occurred in ancient Israel. God's people of old were a fellowship, a family, bound together by racial descent. Their corporate identity was a beautiful and powerful thing and gave them an enormous advantage. For they did not think of themselves as individuals except with reference to the family. A man called himself by the name of his father, and that implied a whole ancestry going back to Abraham. Nobody thought of taking a census of individuals. What they counted was adult males, and that was in effect a counting of family units. Nobody thought that women were somehow being discriminated against just because circumcision was limited to males, so tight was the sense of unity in marriage.

The solidarity of the family is behind texts that speak of God's visiting the iniquity of fathers upon the children (Ex. 20:5). Even a horrible story like that of Jehu's slaughter of the whole house of Ahab, 70 sons, testifies to the powerful conception of family unity (2 Kings 10). A man was not really dead unless his whole family had been cut off with him.

Children were thought of as being still in the womb of home and family until the day came when a young man went out from one house and a young woman from another and they established a new home. The day of marriage was the day of maturity, the completion of the birth of them both. The Law stressed the obedience of children to parents, for the parents stood over against their children in the place of God, while the parents continued to stand over against God in the place of children. Thus God was the head of every family, and the Father of the whole family of Israel.

Therefore education centered in the family. Education in the law of the Lord occurred in and through family worship and celebration. The whole family was involved in the feast of bringing the firstfruits to the LORD. At the Feast of Booths the whole family down to the smallest child slept out for a week in crude lean-to shelters, in remembrance of the wanderings of their fathers in the wilderness and as a reminder that all the blessings of the land came to them for nothing, in sheer fulfillment of the divine promise (Lev. 23:39-43). So also the Feast of the Passover and with it of Unleavened Bread carried the family back to Egypt, to the night of departure from slavery (Ex. 12). As they ate the lamb and the bread and drank the wine of fulfillment, the child would ask what it all meant (Ex. 12:26). Then would follow the retelling of the whole history of the covenant, with its meaning for the present identity of this family and all the tribes and families of Israel as the chosen people of God, called out of this world and into holiness. When a new male child was born into the home, the octave of his birthday was the day of his circumcision and naming, an occasion of great public joy and celebration in remembrance of God's grace to His people.

It was families who watched out for strangers and for widows and orphans whose own families had been broken. For it was by the gift of the LORD that the solitary were set in families (Ps. 68:5-6) and the barren woman was blessed with children (Ps. 113:9). The whole imagery magnifies the grace of God, the liberal freedom of His mercy. For the woman is God's great gift to the man. Children are a gift of God to parents. No child asks to be born or has his place in the home out of some will or achievement of his own. It is all the gift of God, the product of God's determination. The future belongs to the child not by right of achievement but by right of inheritance. At home he does not have to compete in order to achieve some status. He has the status, as a gift. He is the son and heir. That is given to him. And what the child has within the family, Israel has in relation to God. Therefore life consists in singing hallelujahs, in worshipful remembering and repeating of the family history and identity, in obedience and service to God and the brother. Tomorrow is secure in the hands of God, and His people wait to receive it from Him.

The imagery of the New Testament church stands directly on the history and experience of Old Testament Israel. There are differences, of course. Through the death and resurrection of Jesus the old covenant has passed away. The identifying mark of God's people now is no longer racial descent from Abraham or circumcision or observance of distinctively Jewish ordinances like the Sabbath or distinctions of meats. It is rather baptism into the name of Jesus Christ, into His sonship and identity as the fulfillment of the old covenant. The breakthrough has occurred. "The Gentiles are fellow heirs, members of the same body, and partakers of the promise in Christ Jesus through the Gospel," as Saint Paul says (Eph. 3:6). The great stumbling block for the Jew is that he must himself wear the wedding garment of Baptism

(Matt. 22:11-14), count all his old claims to the Kingdom as dung (Phil. 3:8), and thus belong to the people of God exactly as the Gentiles do — by grace, through Christ alone.

Nevertheless the church, like Israel of old, is the family of God's people. The Gentiles are no longer strangers in chance contact with Jews. They *belong!* They are fellow citizens with the saints, members of the household of God (Eph. 2:19). Thus the name "Father" for God attaches now not only to the limited race of Israel but to "every family in heaven and on earth" (Eph. 3:15). Families are important in the church, just as they were in Israel of old. Peter on Pentecost declares, "The promise is to you and to your children" (Acts 2:39). Worship goes on not only in the temple but in the homes (Acts 2:46). Baptism takes in entire households (Acts 16:15, 31-32; John 4:53). When St. Paul urges fathers to bring up their children in the nurture and instruction of the Lord (Eph. 6:4), his imagery draws on the family piety of old Israel. When he describes the church as the glorious bride of Christ (Eph. 5:25-27), this too rests on the Old Testament picture of Yahweh as the Husband of Israel (Is. 54:1-7; 62:4-5). The church is made up of families, husbands and wives and their children, drawn together in the Spirit into the larger family and fellowship by their one hope, one Lord, one faith, one baptism, one God and Father of all. (Eph. 4:4-6)

In the family and fellowship of the church, Christian education occurs. It is in the family that the words of Gospel and promise make their greatest sense, for the family situation affirms the principle of grace alone. When neighborhood children become destructive, we put them out of the yard. When it comes to our own children, however, though we may chastise them, we do not put them out. The very situation underscores the freedom of the Gospel and of the sonship and promises of God. The door of the house is open to the family that lives there. It provides access to the Father.

The home is the one place where identity has meaning apart from achievement. The child got his name for nothing; he did not make it for himself. Out in the world every child learns that his worth is measured solely by what he does. If he commits an error for the ball team or strikes out with the bases loaded, he is a bum. If he makes a sterling play or drives in the winning run, he is a hero. Only in the home is he free to be loved for nothing. Similarly for the Christian the measure of his identity is neither his achievement nor his failure as men judge these things, but the Word of God and the promises with which God surrounds his life. Under that Word there is no place for either boasting or despair, for classifications like "superior" or "inferior." There is only the call and the glory of belonging to the family, the family of God.

Thus Christian education occurs within and capitalizes on the family-fellowship of God's holy people. For that reason it capitalizes also on the sacraments. The whole question of identity, hope, and present calling is summed up in Baptism, as we have seen. Therefore, in a sense, all of Christian education is an exposition of Baptism.

But Holy Communion is equally in the picture. The oldest tradition of Christendom suggests that children received not only Baptism but also the Lord's Supper from infancy. That ancient practice, still familiar in Eastern Orthodoxy, seems curiously consistent with the Gospel, for it is clear then that the food of the Sacrament, like Baptism, is altogether a divine gift. As a child does not choose to be born, he does not choose to be baptized either. Life, both physical and spiritual, is simply *given* him, by grace alone. "Freedom" does not include the possibility of refusing birth (though Hos. 13:12-13 does explore that thought). Similarly a little baby does not choose whether he will or will not *eat*. The milk that sustains him within the family is given him,

80

and he accepts it eagerly and without question. He does not have to be aware of his life in order to live, or understand diet and metabolic processes in order to benefit from the milk he sucks. By analogy, then, the tradition of offering an infant the Sacrament of the body and blood of Christ simply by right of his new birth in Baptism would make Holy Communion the means of his immediate and continuing nurture long before he could understand intellectually what either Sacrament means. In practice a child would no more remember when he started receiving Communion than he would remember when he was born, or baptized, or when he first sucked milk.

In our traditional Lutheran practice we have not operated with this analogy, but have withheld the Sacrament from children until they have been instructed and confirmed. Our procedure deserves the reexamination it has been receiving, above all because it leads so readily to a distorted conception of the Gospel. We insist, of course, that salvation and every gift of God is ours by grace alone. Nevertheless the children we teach cannot quite escape the impression that the privilege of the Sacrament is theirs as a kind of reward for achievement. For our custom has been to welcome them to the Lord's altar, as a right and privilege of "communicant" membership in the congregation, only when they have fulfilled the requirement of instruction and then been confirmed.[4]

An argument from analogy can be precarious, of course. The question is whether the Bible itself offers any encouragement for the possibility that Holy Communion has the aspect of a sacrament of nurture, following Baptism as the sacrament of new birth. The evidence is indirect, but sufficient to merit consideration. The Lord's Supper is a sacrificial meal, founded in the context of one of the great Old Testament sacrificial meals, the Passover (Ex. 12; Matt. 26:2,

17-29; 1 Cor. 5:7). But a sacrificial meal, the Passover included (Ex. 12:26), was never reserved as a prerogative of adults only. It was a family celebration, and the children participated. According to 1 Sam. 1, Elkanah took his whole family to the annual feast of the LORD at Shiloh and gave portions of the sacrifice to them all. When Samuel was an infant, Hannah chose to miss the feast until he was weaned, for then she would leave him at Shiloh to grow up in the presence of the LORD. The assumption was that a weaned child, once off its mother's breast, was old enough to participate in the sacrificial worship even to the point of eating the sacrifice. This perspective is preserved in the practice of Eastern Orthodoxy, where a child after Baptism is immediately introduced to Holy Communion and made a participant in the body and blood of Christ by eating a fragment of bread dipped in the wine. Whatever the warnings of 1 Cor. 11:27-29 mean, they cannot possibly imply that little children who came to worship with their families in Corinth were not to eat of the Holy Sacrament because they had not yet been informed intellectually what this food was. The problem St. Paul addresses is an adult problem, not a problem of the children.

So we need to get the horse before the cart again. In Israel the celebration of feasts and sacrifices was the occasion of education. A child participated; he was concretely and altogether in on it. Then came the rehearsal of the history, the public remembering of what it was all about. So Jesus says: "Do this in remembrance of Me." That is His invitation to *do it* and in doing it to *teach from it*. Here is the great chance to repeat the story—how Jesus fulfilled His sonship and obedience to His Father by laying down His life for us. Here we declare how different the church is from the world, by showing how different Jesus was in His holiness. For He did not live by calculation of consequences or by devising

82

clever strategies in difficult situations so as to achieve the greatest good at the cost of the least evil. His wisdom was to do the will of the Father and to entrust the whole business of purpose and outcome to Him. Therefore He drank the cup of suffering, which He invites us to drink in His own blood, and ate the bread of affliction, which the church too is not afraid to eat as it participates in the body of His death. But God raised Him from the dead and declared to the end of the age that the wisdom of those who pray, "Hallowed be Thy name, Thy kingdom come, Thy will be done on earth" is greater than all the wisdom of the world.

Thus Christian education must derive from and give expression to the fellowship and the worship of the church. It takes the children where they are, in their identity within the people of God, and it unfolds to them the personal history of their own unique humanity. It declares constantly that the child will find his true individuality and uniqueness as he sees himself in relation to God and to God's people and to humanity as a whole. The biography of the child is not only his own brief and immediate history and environment but the entire biography of humankind. Therefore the history of Jesus and of Old Testament Israel belongs to his personal history. The story of the holy infection which God the Father is working in the world against such obstacles, that story anticipates the child's personal biography.

But this means that Christian education must constantly stand in contrast to the world. Everything it says must be alive to the contrast. The church is thoroughly realistic. Its children belong to the humanity that knows good and evil. Their natural flesh stands in full sympathy with their world. That is why even Christian children feel the exhilaration of success, and the terrible burden of accusation and failure, and the numb plodding of those who are always somewhere in the middle, never total failures but never gloriously successful either. And these children of ours must understand that this is how the world operates. The grading system in school, the inevitable ranking of children in terms of relative popularity, the experience of victory and defeat in athletic competition — all this belongs to the world in which they are called to live and from which they must not even try to escape. For the world will indeed measure them only by their achievements. It will exalt some and ignore or even degrade others. That is the only way the world can respond, for it is bound to react out of its knowledge of good and evil. Rather than hide this reality or protect its children from it, the Christian school ought to capitalize on every manifestation of it so as to help them understand what that world is like in which they live and will live, and how the power of its thinking works also in their own natural hearts.

But these children must know too that the very system of "knowing good and evil" is under judgment. Those who attempt to build their lives on such wisdom are erecting their houses on sand rather than rock (Matt. 7:24-27). Though God requires men to live by their usurped wisdom, it belongs to the form of the world that is passing away (1 Cor. 7:29-31). The children of God accept their Father's call to continue living in such a world, but they also have a mighty secret in themselves, the secret wisdom of being little children of the heavenly Father and knowing their Father in Jesus Christ. By that wisdom they, as children of God, are restored to God's image and likeness. They are above the knowledge of good and evil even while they must work and live within it. They know that good and evil in the ultimate sense is beyond the wisdom of man. Only the blind and arrogant boast as though man could actually succeed in being like God in probing the future, in performing those actions now that will result in the greatest good for himself and an escape from evil. The judgment of death rests on all such wisdom and calculation.

84

But to know, love, trust, and fear God alone—that is the beginning of true wisdom. For then a man is measured by what God says of him, not by what the world thinks. And then he has a treasure that even death cannot destroy. Out of this unique glory and security of the child of God come the power and vision to fulfill his life in freedom and obedience to his Father, in love and service to his brothers, and as a holy infection toward the world.

In the relativism of men, Christian education preserves and transmits the eternal truth. The church must not, therefore, capitulate to contemporary relativism. We have more to do for our youth than to squeeze their hand in silent sympathy while each of them goes through the hell of trying to find himself, of rationalizing some place to stand that will satisfy his private yearnings. The church has better things to do than to conform to the world's relativistic language and adopt the idiom of the day in order to demonstrate how well it understands the problem.

Christian education has one resource, the eternal truth of the Gospel. It has one task, to nurture the next generation in the life of that Gospel so that our youth may be an infection of God's life to a world dying of its own arrogance, to a generation in despair because it feels it must move the earth and yet can find no place to stand.

4

In the Calculation of Men —
The Foolishness of the Cross (Service)

We all know that, whatever Christian service may mean, it occurs in the context of the secular world. I shall not belabor the point, because I do not see any serious ambiguity or doubt in the church today regarding it.

In Luther's time, of course, the concept was almost revolutionary. Christians then attributed a greater holiness to asceticism, to withdrawal from the world, to works of special religious devotion, to the commitment of men to vows and sacred orders. Poverty was more holy than wealth, chastity more holy than sexuality, obedience to the pope more holy than obedience to an employer or prince. It was more holy to leave your property to the church than to your children, to be a monk than to be a lawyer or farmer. Religious orders assumed the task of expressing the holiness of the church in ways in which ordinary secular people could not express it. Against such a distortion Luther summoned people to take the world and their calling in it seriously. He himself left the monastery, entered the world again, took a wife and had children. The world was a great place to be because God had put man there and continually poured out on him the earth's benefits.

Thus the holiness of the Christian today does not pull him out of the world but sends him into it. The Christian is a citizen and takes seriously his calling in relation to the state. He has a role in his family, whether as husband or wife, parent or child. He is either an employer or an employee. Read the Table of Duties connected to the Small Catechism, and the sets of Biblical texts cited there. The Christian is a very normal person as he moves within the society around him. He finds his role by way of the opportunities that open to him or sometimes by taking seriously and pressing toward his own special interests, inclinations, and gifts. He will indeed see the guiding hand of God in all this. He will also notice when the path he has chosen is blocked, and may well turn in a new direction in the confidence that the Lord God is turning him. He may experience vocational uncertainties. But wherever he is, there is work to be done, and he receives this very work from God as a call to serve his Father, that is, to act by applying all the powers God has given him. He is summoned to use and develop his skills of mind and hand to the fullest potential. He thinks hard and works hard. He takes home his pay. He enjoys the pleasures of life, receiving them with thanksgiving. He lives in society and stands shoulder to shoulder with the secular humanity to which he belongs. He enjoys friendships. In all these things and many more, he is thoroughly in the world and a part of it. Such a wholesome outlook on the world is reflected in the whole of Biblical history and theology.

In another sense too the Christian stands squarely in the world, even in the fallen world, and shoulder to shoulder with his secular brethren. He lives by the knowledge of good and evil, that is, by prudential wisdom and thoroughly secular common sense. Thus we look over our homes to make them as safe as possible, on the principle that "an ounce of prevention is worth a pound of cure." We anticipate the possibility of potential catastrophe and guard against it by buying insurance to the extent we are able. We learn the art and necessity of living within our income. We encourage our children to "grow up," that is, to develop a more responsible and refined knowledge of good and evil. For it may look like lots of fun to ram one another at full speed on their bicycles or at least to pretend to do so, but it just is not common sense. The hazards of life, limb, and property are excessive. We hide the matches. We impose our knowledge of good and evil on the children. Much as they dislike shots and vaccines, we force them to accept such "evils" in the interest of the greater and long-range good. The Christian man who buys stocks draws on the best experience, his own and others, to make a sound investment. The druggist who debates whether to put in a new line of merchandise proposed to him by some salesman makes his decision on the basis of advantage versus disadvantage, good versus evil. In all this the Christian is not essentially different from his secular neighbor.

There is sound Biblical authority for such good and evil decision-making on the part of God's holy people. Here again the Bible is altogether realistic and down to earth. God in no way demands that we sprout some kind of angelic wings to lift ourselves by faith above that sort of thing. The story of the Fall does not suggest that man can return to the garden of God, even though God has spoken to him and has had mercy on him. Though the clothing he devised for himself is inadequate and even ridiculous, man cannot go back to being naked. The LORD Himself makes garments of skins for the man and the woman, and clothes them (Gen. 3:21). Leather is, of course, more durable as clothing than fig leaves. Yet the real durability lies in the fact that God makes this clothing for them. They do not improvise it for themselves. The garment of skins signals the righteousness God's people have freely from God in the forgiveness of sins. (Is. 61:10)

But it also signals the fact that the man and his wife must now live in the condition of fallenness. As surely as the people of God do not escape the sweat, pain, frustration, and dust of the humanity to which they belong, so surely can they not escape the necessity of calculating consequences and determining their actions by the kind of wisdom men thought would make them to be like God. To try to escape this now would, in fact, be further rebellion. Man cannot cure himself of the Fall or defy shame and death by deciding to go nude. Apart from the fact that the shame over nakedness in the Biblical account has to do not so much with the feelings of Adam and Eve toward each other as with their posture before God, nudism, if there is any theological motive at all behind it, is defiance. For repentance and submission to God is now demonstrated precisely in accepting the new reality, submitting to the verdict of God, wearing clothes, and living by the practical wisdom of knowing good and evil.

A parallel story would be that of Kadesh-barnea. After Israel had heard the judgment of God that they must wander in the wilderness until that whole generation died, some of them, admitting their sin, rallied courageously as though to storm the land of Canaan anyhow, and were immediately destroyed (Num. 14). That was again defiance masquerading as repentance. We are not called to change our situation under God's judgment but to trust Him by accepting the terms of His verdict. In doing so, however, we paradoxically leave the knowledge of good and evil to God even while we continue to live by it. Incidentally, there is a clear warning here against any false defense of old fortresses in the name of faith, under the assumption that our God cannot change His way of doing things. Biblical history shows that God can change His ways and quite often does, always to the confusion of those who thought they had somehow contained and controlled Him and made Him predictable.

Thus whatever it is that marks the Christian as holy and different in the world, it is not some strange escape from secularity or some supernatural freedom from the necessity of calculating consequences by wisdom for the best personal advantage.

We may go one step further. The Christian is not different in the sense that he serves his neighbor while the secular man does not. Christians have no monopoly on service, not even, in a sense, on love. The Gentile and the tax collector are quite capable of loving, Jesus concedes (Matt. 5:46-47), and of greeting the people they meet in a friendly way. For lives of service can be produced completely within and by the knowledge of good and evil.

When we were children we learned from experience that it does not pay to be selfish or to let our selfishness show too much. For our brothers and sisters and playmates were selfish too, and they just could not allow us to achieve any kind of personal advantage over them. They even understood the Law. "You shouldn't be so selfish," they could say very perceptively. So we all learned to settle for justice, for equality in relation to other people. If we respected the rights of others, we could justly claim the right to have our own rights respected. Though we would prefer to have had our own way in everything, we accepted justice as our best out, and in unity with our fellows exalted it as the highest good. Thus, if anybody began to get the upper hand over us, we could cry, "Help! Justice!" and the world would come running to serve and save us from the bully who was trying to overpower us. At least we hoped it would. If it didn't, we could nurse our grudges in bitterness at being treated so unjustly. Justice is great when you can get it going for you. Of course even the bully can lay some claim to "justice," as when the child who is beating another says, "But he hit me first!"

In such a way the knowledge of good and evil can make servants out of people. By it we learn to be modest, for if our achievements make other people feel inferior, they reward us not with compliments but with brickbats. Modesty is the technique of keeping our superiority discreetly hidden, for fear of other people. Of course we do hope that somebody will notice and advertise our superiority for us. Other standard virtues pay off too—for instance, patience and a little generosity now and then. And if we have been guilty of hurting somebody, we can sometimes retrieve his favor by artfully apologizing or by doing him some service or by offering to let him satisfy his resentment by hitting us in the arm as hard as he wants to. In the high art of living with other people, the knowledge of good and evil has much to contribute.

So it is also with service: "Service is our middle name"; "Service with a smile"; "We service what we sell." Even a loan company comforts us in our financial distress by the promise of its speedy and friendly service. Hertz ads have assured us that if we are going to suffer minor catastrophes, like losing a wallet, getting a piece of grit in our eye, or having a toothache in a strange land, we are very fortunate if the Hertz agency is the place it happens. Service is available all over the place, and we have much occasion to be grateful for it. It is a great convenience to run out of gas within coasting range of a service station, and to have the tires and oil checked and windshield cleaned besides.

But we all know that this is business. We pay $2.50 for a haircut and say thanks for the service, and we pay the union plumber $8.50 an hour and say thanks for the service. But we don't kid ourselves. If we Christians are barbers or plumbers, or run a loan company or gas station, we know that our service is not any kind of Christian testimony. And if anybody begins to overdo the service bit, like the politician

91

who says once too often, "I'm only here to serve you," we even find ourselves reacting in cynicism, because we know that the knowledge of good and evil can produce service. Even children in Christian homes have been known to do their best work of service not out of any great and free self-offering love but when they are either bribed with money or threatened with wrath. Their knowledge of good and evil is a powerful thing.

The knowledge of good and evil can produce service in more subtle ways, of course. It can contribute to the art of winning friends and influencing people. It can be a cover for guilt, a kind of self-atonement, as when a gangster, adopting a posture of suburban respectability, donates liberally to public and private causes. The desire to suppress the pea of guilt under 24 layers of mattresses is powerful in all of us. That was, after all, what drove young Luther into the monastery. People will serve too if you flatter them enough, or if by serving they can enhance a public image, or if they can just get that persistent widow away from the door and go back to sleep (Luke 18:1-5), or if they cannot graciously get out of it, the cost of refusal being greater than the cost of participation.

Perhaps the most subtle force that can drive people to service under the knowledge of good and evil is their compelling need to justify their own existence, to find some kind of worth and value in being alive, or simply to be noticed and approved rather than lost in the crowd and ignored. This sort of thing can stimulate youth to a high idealism. It drives many of them into the Peace Corps, where they do great and noble work and where they find great satisfactions and fulfillment. It spurs bright young people to train for professions that will not necessarily yield them the most returns in the form of money and comfort and a well-ordered routine with lots of leisure time. They want to do something to "help people," they say, and so they go into teaching or social work or nursing or some such thing. What I am saying is that all this can happen within natural man, within the secular world, within the knowledge of good and evil. You don't have to be a Christian in order to be motivated to help people or love a neighbor.

So what is the holiness, the *differentness*, about Christian service that makes it salt in the earth and a light in the world? It is pretty hard to see. We may argue, "I do it for Christian love, the other fellow for motives that are ultimately self-centered and calculating, whether he realizes it or not. I am acting out of the knowledge of God, he out of the knowledge of good and evil." But does that hold up? For one thing, how is the person you serve going to detect the difference? Will you smile more than the other guy or be more patient than he or maybe respect the other fellow as a person more than he? Why, secular social work knows all about this. To respect the other person, to love him and relate to him, and to do everything possible to really help him are all part of professional competence. As a matter of fact, what you display as Christian love could very well louse up the whole business of helping him. Well then, how does the distinctive holiness of Christian service show? Is it that we wear a clerical collar or a little cross on some kind of uniform? But surely the collar and the cross don't make the service Christian!

There is another complication. Our own motives are so desperately impure. We don't act out of the wisdom of good and evil simply by God's command. We do it out of our total natural fleshly instinct. I was talking about my own children when I said that they work best when they are either threatened or bribed. And when they do begin to grow up and take a more willing and responsible role, I still don't know whether it is Christian love or secular maturity

93

that is doing it. I don't even know that in myself. I go through moods. I love to be exhilarated, I hate to be depressed. I find that I am exhilarated when I can point to evidences that I count for something, and that I am depressed when the evidences have doubtful value or even point to my worthlessness. But I know very well that both my exhilaration and my depression are the product of my natural knowledge of good and evil.

Let's not kid ourselves about the holiness of our desires to serve the Lord and men. A man can achieve success in the holy ministry just as in any other profession. He can feel important and respected and wanted. He can get income and drive an air-conditioned car and live in a nice suburban house and get a vacation. If he gets to lecture at a camp, he can even get a vacation free. So what's especially Christian or holy about his service? I am not saying all this to be cynical but only to be as coldly realistic as possible and to destroy any sentimental illusions.

But now, what conclusions may we draw so far from such an analysis? I suggest three:

1. The Christian must not disparage the service that secular men render to our world. He ought rather to welcome it, rejoice in it, and see and accept it as a work of God in the fallen world. In this context it is not the Christian's business to demand purity of motives but only to thank the Lord that in a world fallen from Him God still gets people to serve one another. The service of man to man is a work and gift of God, just as is government and all secular orders of society. As we pray for God to give us good government, so we pray for good neighbors, even if they are not Christians. And when we see such service, we have every cause to compliment and thank and encourage those who perform it, and even to join them in the help they are rendering. If a car is stalled in front of your house and you join your secular neighbor in giving

a push, your push is not better than his just because you are a Christian.

2. The Christian in serving his fellowman applies exactly the same kind of wisdom to the situation as his secular neighbor does. Perhaps the Christian will on occasion remind himself that the intelligence he brings to bear on the problem is a gift of God. Yet as far as *using* that intelligence is concerned, there is no discernible difference. The question is simply, "What can you do in the given circumstance and need, within the limits of your capacity and resources, that will do the most good?" The question calls for wisdom, experience, study, evidence, hard and imaginative thinking, willingness to take a risk, anticipation of alternative consequences — in short, everything having to do with knowing good and evil.

This is exactly the kind of thing our courageous and imaginative brethren who have dared to move in on the overwhelming problems of our inner cities have been doing. God bless them! But the Christian who is mayor of a city or a physician or a legislator also has the kind of summons to think wisely and responsibly in service to his fellowmen, to weigh alternatives and calculate consequences. I would go further and suggest that the Christian physician or legislator must be free to act out of his prudential knowledge of good and evil even against what may seem to be a Biblical moral law. For example, suppose the legislature of a state is tormented with the question of legalizing therapeutic abortions. I do not see how the church can take any other position in such a matter than to tell the Christian legislator to join his non-Christian colleague in working out the wisest law possible, anticipating as well as can be done every potential consequence, altogether according to their common knowledge of good and evil — and then to pray for them both. This, of course, is what the whole business of situation ethics is all about. Notice that it is possible for the knowledge of good and evil to be applied in such cases entirely apart from any personal stake that the legislators may have in the matter. They may not be dealing with what is good and evil specifically for themselves, but for society as a whole, for others. That is the way they do their serving.

3. Since Christian service is not distinguishable from secular service, it does not witness to Christ. To call the service enterprise a Christian "witness," or to justify it on the ground that it is a form of preaching, only creates confusion. Christian service needs no such justification. In past centuries Christians saw the need for hospitals, orphanages, and institutions for the care of the aged. Today the church is being drawn into depressed areas, to minister to the economically and socially disadvantaged. The struggle is under way to determine what must be done and the most effective procedures for getting it done. The call to respond to obvious human need and suffering with all wisdom, love, and imagination has a validity of its own quite apart from the "opportunity for witness." If the Holy Spirit has moved and driven some of our brethren to pioneer in such new dimensions of service, the rest of us ought to support their work with our prayers, gifts, and sometimes counsel. But we ought not to judge the validity of such work in terms of the amount of Gospel that is preached or the number of souls won. Conversely these brethren ought not to feel constrained to defend the validity of their work by claiming that an act of love itself preaches the Gospel.

Let service be service, and witness witness. Christian activity in serving the suffering of the world has a sufficient glory of its own simply as a response to a cry of need. It is consistent with the Gospel as an expression of love. But service as such does not proclaim Christ or reveal God, for it cannot set men free of the knowledge of good and evil, which constitutes their ultimate imprisonment.. However, since both service and witness happen in the church (just as do worship, fellowship, and education), we may expect that the one will inevitably overflow into the other. The man whose specific call is to serve will find his mouth opened also to witnessing, as did "servants" like Stephen and Philip, who quickly became evangelists (Acts 6—8). On the other hand, the man whose explicit mission is to preach continually finds himself confronted by human needs and the call to serve.

I have made the distinction between witness and service deliberately, even offensively, sharp. It has seemed necessary to do this in order to magnify the importance of the spoken Word in the vapid theological climate of our time. For there are theologians, akin to the "enthusiasts" of Luther's day, who expect that the Spirit of God will be imparted and the love of God made known even without words, if only we perform acts of love and establish relationships between people which create their own kind of healing. In such a climate, they imagine, an intuitive knowledge of God's presence and care will permeate men, and not only through Christianity but in all religions. But in all this there is no diagnosis of the inherent ungodliness of men, no understanding of the sin that imprisons, deceives, and kills, no repentance, no Christ, no sacrament, no words that open up a new world of light and life and freedom in the sonship that clothes us through the forgiveness of sins. For it is very clear, in John 6 for example, that the bread Jesus multiplied in the wilderness out of compassion for the hungry could no more give them eternal life than could the manna their fathers had eaten. The true bread from heaven is the "word that proceeds out of the mouth of the LORD" (Deut. 8:3), in this instance the gory Word God speaks in Christ crucified. "Unless you eat the flesh of the Son of Man and drink His blood, you have no life in you" (John 6:53). "The words that I have spoken to you are spirit and life." (John 6:63)

Once it is clear that Christ, the Spirit, and the knowledge of the Father come only by Word and Sacrament, we may without fear of distortion acknowledge those texts that point to actions as an element in witness. For it is certainly assumed that he who speaks the Word of the Gospel loves his hearers and that his whole bearing and action will support his testimony. The disciples who, like the prophets of old, endure persecution for their witness to Jesus will also "shine before men" with their "good works" (Matt. 5:13-16). Christian wives whose husbands have rejected the Word may yet win them "without a word" by their "reverent and chaste behavior" (1 Peter 3:1). Jesus' own obedience, in the context of His whole preaching and action, especially His surrender to the death of the cross, speaks the Word of God so powerfully that He Himself is explicitly called "the Word." (John 1:1-3)

There is another side to the picture, however. If the service the Christian renders to his fellowman is not visibly different from that rendered by his non-Christian but morally decent neighbor, nevertheless the Christian is a different kind of person. This differentness can and does affect his serving.

For one thing, he is not trying to be "like God" when he operates with the knowledge of good and evil. He is acting rather in submission and obedience to God. He accepts the situation of the fallen world and is willing to live within fallen humanity. Thus the determinative wisdom for his life is the fear of the Lord, not the knowledge of good and evil. The secular neighbor is creating his own life and assuring himself of his own worth even by the things he does for his neighbor. That is his idolatry. But the man in Christ leaves the business of his identity and destiny to his

98

heavenly Father. Therefore if he experiences blessings, he thanks God and does not credit these to his wisdom and work. The glory is always God's.

Second, though the Christian thinks hard to devise the strategy that will best get at the human problem he is facing, he places no ultimate confidence in his knowledge of good and evil, or for that matter in anybody else's. The world is not going to be saved by the wisdom or strength of men, for example, of rulers and governments. "It is better to take refuge in the LORD than to put confidence in man. It is better to take refuge in the LORD than to put confidence in princes," says Ps. 118:8-9. Jer. 17:5 is even stronger. "Thus says the LORD: 'Cursed is the man who trusts in man and makes flesh his arm, whose heart turns away from the LORD!' " The strategies of men have a way of backfiring to destroy those who make them. Ahaz of Judah, when attacked by the petty alliance of Ephraim (northern Israel) and Syria, did not listen to Isaiah's call to trust the Lord. Instead he sent a large gift to the rising giant, Assyria, inviting her to attack his enemies from the rear. It was a great idea, except that Assyria did not stop after destroying Syria and Ephraim but swept right on to devour Judah too, devastating her in what may have been two separate invasions under Hezekiah and holding her under crushing tyranny for a century. The cure turned out to be far worse than the sickness, just as Isaiah had predicted. (Is. 7)

Now this sort of thing happens all the time, almost as though the LORD in heaven were laughing at the devices of men and continually spoofing their best wisdom. It seems a great good to use vast quantities of chemicals for insect control, yet Michigan has now banned the use of DDT after finding that the mosquito plague it had once controlled is worse than ever, for the chemical has succeeded in killing off the mosquito's natural enemies even more than destroy-

99

ing the mosquito itself. It seems good that we should have great factories to produce all the benefits and comforts of modern life for us, yet now we have lakes we cannot swim or fish in, and we face the fearful threat of poisoned water and poisoned air. It seems good that medical science should enable us to live so much longer and so much more comfortably, and we have with great generosity exported our medical progress on a worldwide scale. But now the threat of exploding populations is upon us. It seems good therefore that medical science should come up with the solution to that one too, namely "the pill," but I'm a skeptic like Isaiah. Quite apart from untested medical consequences, this presumption of wisdom may harbor hidden folly. For example, the sophisticated calculation of the wise will now deny conception to the fourth (or ninth) child, who often in the past has proved an exceptional blessing to mankind. Who knows whether families will be happier or the world better? I cannot help but think of ancient Rome. It seemed good to Roman social nobility to drink wine out of luxurious and finely crafted leaden cups. But it has taken a millennium and a half to discover why the cream of the Roman population for more than two centuries kept dying off in their early thirties. It was lead poisoning that did it, the evil hidden in the good.

It seemed good to us in 1954, when the French withdrew from a partitioned Vietnam, that a token American presence be established in southeast Asia as a wall against Communist aggression, but who ever dreamt that this little investment would suck into itself such an enormity of cost in wealth and blood and division and frustration! And when people shout, "We gotta get out!" and, "Stop the bombing!" on the one hand, and, "Let's not fight a limited war!" and, "Bomb Haiphong!" on the other, then we begin to taste the dread and torment that can be involved when we know that we must know good and evil and yet cannot

100

know. If ever there is a time for Christians to pray for their President, to urge him to make the best decisions he can, and then throw ourselves on the mercy of our God, this is such a time! Only Christians can pray that way, because we know that we don't know!

Again, it seems good to us that wise men representing the nations of the world should gather in a United Nations to look at the large questions of good and evil from the broadest perspective of the whole race. And yet there are times when we wonder whether the unity of mankind represented here is worth a hoot. The speeches make it very clear that the self-interest of each nation has the primacy. Maybe the wisest thing to do in international disputes is to lay off, let the combatants slug it out in bloody combat, and allow the victor the privilege of dictating the terms of peace. Maybe a bloody war like that of Israel against the Arab alliance is the best hope of an enduring peace in a world in which men and nations are dead set against one another in their passion for the good and their hatred of evil. A war can perhaps be more merciful in the long run than desperate and artificial efforts of "wise" men to prevent it. Who knows what is good and what is evil? That is the kind of question the Christian can and must address to every arrogance of man.

One further illustration. It strikes me that the most ironic dilemma in which the knowledge of good and evil has involved American society derives from nothing less than the American dream. The dream, of course, is good. The dream cries, "Equal opportunity for all," and within this so-called land of opportunity it encourages every man to "get ahead." In the name of opportunity and getting ahead we encourage our youth not to be high school dropouts but to get the best education possible so that they can serve not only themselves but their country. Anybody can achieve wealth or station in this great land of ours, we say, if he turns his imagination loose and is willing to work. Now it is difficult at first hand to argue with that essential thesis. It is not founded on any hypothetical political or economic or social philosophy but is down to earth in its realism. It matches a basic human drive — to be somebody, to be important, to make something of oneself. The American climate of maximum freedom keeps the dream alive. The success of the system is evident in the spectacular progress America has made. No land has ever come so close to achieving the dream of Babel, the hand of man touching the stars.

And yet the dream, great as it is, generates its own poison. Enjoy the wine, you rich and prosperous people, but you are drinking from a leaden cup! Because to "get ahead" always means to leave somebody else behind. The farther ahead any man gets, the more people he has left behind. Perhaps the great middle class doesn't feel this quite so much. To be in the middle class means that certain people have gotten ahead of you, but then, you haven't done too badly either. You can boast of moderate progress, at least toward limited dreams. But what of those who are left way behind? What of those who could not compete, who were frozen out from the beginning by a complexity of internal and external forces? What happens to those for whom the cry, "Get ahead!" comes through as nothing but an impossible demand, a taunt, and an accusation? What about them?

I learned about this from my children. When one had been in first grade for a month, her sister asked, "Who is the brightest in your class?" Immediately the child mentioned a name. "Who is the second brightest?" She knew that too. She also classified herself as fifth in the class, and she knew who was the dumbest and next to the dumbest. I confess that I was astounded. Our school doesn't give grades, but it doesn't have to. The children have a pretty fair idea of where every member of the class stands.

But this got me to thinking about that child at the very bottom of the class. As he goes on through school and becomes more and more conscious of his position, what happens to him? Even the second from the bottom has a certain consolation, for he can say, "At least I'm not the worst one." I've heard that line in our family too. But what about the bottom child? Children can be very cruel. If the bottom child looks or talks funny in addition to being the dumbest, they let him know. Then he is forced to develop compensations by which to prove that he is worth something, or he must deaden the pain by hardening himself and hiding. He can retreat into dreams. He can protect himself against the next failure by not even trying, for if he does not play the game, he at least cannot be defeated. What does the "land of opportunity" or the cry, "Get ahead!" mean to him?

That is why we must have slums and depressed areas. That is why we have people around, though we like to keep them out of our sight, who have been defeated so often long ago that they cannot be brought out of their shells any more to make another venture. That is why sexual lust or drink or dope becomes so ready a compensation for men and women whose inadequacies terrify them. For every man on the top there must be one on the bottom. To get ahead means to pass the other man by. To move to the suburbs means to leave the other man in the city. And nothing reveals the depth of the sickness quite as effectively as to hear a man who has made his way upward shout the gospel of the American dream to those still on the bottom and say, "Come on! I made it; so can you!" or who curses the apathy of those who live in the bondage of their paralysis and says, "Why don't they get to work?"

103

"They sow the wind, and they shall reap the whirl-wind." That was Hosea's way of describing how the man who pursues good will find fearful evil catching up with and overwhelming him (Hos. 8:7). But the wise men of our age don't see this. When the new evil confronts them, they go back to their drawing boards and once again out of the knowledge of good and evil come up with solutions — mammoth federal programs for control of air and water pollution, urban renewal, rigid enforcement of housing codes in the slums, elimination of rats, hospital care and better legal protection for alcoholics, Head Start programs, Job Corps programs, open-housing legislation. All these are "good," we say, and I guess they are.

But how increasingly complex and precarious things get when the knowledge of good and evil is now called upon to undo the evil that accompanied its pursuit of good! Urban renewal looks nice, but what happens to the families whose dwellings were condemned? Antipoverty wars sound great, but where do you find an administrator who will work for less than $18,000 a year and how do you keep the thing from becoming a windfall for politicians? Open housing sounds good, but how do you keep a white man from moving out of a neighborhood when a black family moves next door and how do you make another white man buy his house? Better education in deprived areas is obviously good, but where do you get teachers who have the combination of guts and skill to do this kind of work? And if you've got one, how do you keep an administrator with an excessive sense of his own importance from harassing him? Aid to Dependent Children sounds good, but how do you really convince the recipients that it is not a degrading and paternalistic gift but that they deserve it and have a right to it? Everything sounds good, but how much money can the government spend or are American citizens going to be willing to spend? And how do you know that the good you did by all this will not itself give rise to still another set of unforeseen evils? And when you have done all these things, you are still not down to the root of it. How do you keep the great American dream from being a curse to those on the bottom, whom the stronger and smarter pass by and leave behind on their own way up?

So we are stuck with our knowledge of good and evil, and we must work by it, even we Christians. But the Christian is different in this, at least, that he knows the world is not going to be saved by the wisdom of knowing good and evil, neither his own nor that of his secular neighbor.

Now we come to the final way in which the Christian in his service differs from his secular neighbor, potentially at least. It is this, that when a man knows God in Christ, receives all blessings with a hallelujah, and rests in the words and promises of his Father, he has the power to transcend the knowledge of good and evil. Because he trusts his heavenly Father, he can surrender the question of what is good for himself or what might hurt him. He can say, "Thy will be done on earth," that is, in this earthly me! That means leaving all wise calculating behind and becoming a holy fool, under the foolishness of the Cross.

So now we ought to consider again Abraham's taking his son to Moriah, David against Goliath, Daniel and the lions, the three Jews in the furnace, or all the contrasting stories of Israel's failure. Above all we ought to repeat once more the story of Jesus, the obedient Son, walking to Jerusalem deliberately and with His eyes wide open, knowing full well the horror of the cross, sweating blood in Gethsemane, confessing to His disciples that His soul is sorrowful unto death, and yet saying, "Father, if there is no other way, Thy will be done!"

We add a word on the meaning of discipleship. To

follow Jesus means to surrender the knowledge of good and evil, to give up all calculation, to take up the cross. "Whoever would save his life will lose it, and whoever loses his life for My sake will find it" (Matt. 16:24-25). Oh, how we love life and hang onto it as the greatest good! But that very valuation of life as so high a good comes out of the knowledge of good and evil! Unless you surrender that knowledge, it will destroy you, says Jesus. You will not succeed in saving your life anyhow, no matter how wise you are. So don't be afraid. Put your life into the hands of the Father, who gave it to you in the first place. All good is from Him; therefore let Him direct your life and protect it. Then you will be free to serve God and to love your brother.

But there is no shortcut, no compromise, no retreat from this. "He who loves father or mother . . . son or daughter more than Me is not worthy of Me" (Matt. 10:37). If you put your hand to the plow and then look back in regret at losing what you left behind, you don't qualify for the kingdom of God (Luke 9:62). The problem of a rich man is that he thinks his riches make him big. He wants to wear fancy dress and bring a caravan into the Kingdom with him. Only when he lets it all go can he become small enough to fit through the eye of a needle (Matt. 19:21-26). So if you are going to start calculating, Jesus suggests, don't make a fool of yourself by undertaking what you will not be willing to see through to the end. You had better sue for peace with the king whose forces outnumber yours if you don't dare to stand up to him for fear of getting hurt. It's stupid to start building a tower if you are going to get tired of paying the bills (Luke 14: 25-35). If you cannot give up your calculating for your future and walk with Me even through the valley of the shadow of death, then you cannot be a salt in the world or an infection of life in the body of death. You have to die to the knowledge of good and evil.

Look over all the passages that present the utter radicality and total demand of Jesus' ethics. Everything turns on this single theme. When the Father says, "Do this," the son is to trust the Father, serve Him, and do it. He is not to say, "I'm too tired." He is not to say, "Wait till I get out my slide rule and figure out how much it will cost me." He is not to say, "Look, I kept the Sabbath, I washed my hands before dinner, I brushed my teeth, and I mowed the lawn. What more do You want?" (Luke 17:7-10). No calculation dare come between the Word of God and the obedience of the son. God said, "Let there be light," and there was light. God says to His son and servant, "Do this," and the son does it, without injecting a calculating argument between God's Word and his own response.

No fear of evil, no law or threat, can engender such an obedience. No love of good, by way of bribery or promise of reward, can produce it either. There is only one power that makes such obedience possible — the power of the Gospel. We are the sons of the heavenly Father through Christ! That is our life and dignity, our joy and freedom! Nobody can take that away from us. We have access to our Father. We know Him and constantly talk to Him. We are like little children, holding His hand or upheld on His bosom. The hairs of our head are all numbered. We have a destiny of eternal life, and nobody can kill that, not even if they should kill the body (Matt. 10:26-33). We neither have nor want to have any will or ambition that is not subjected to the will of the Father for us. We have learned to see the world through the eyes of the Father and the Lord Jesus Christ. We know what life is all about. We are not afraid. We can stand up to the big, tough, and threatening people, the mountains of this world, and without regard to their persons say, "Get out of my way, get lost in the bottom of the sea," and the mountain will move for us (Matt. 21:18-22)! We are part of a

107

life and a program bigger than ourselves, a life as big as God, as wise as God, as eternal as God!

Jesus lives! It turned out that the God of Israel was not dead after all when Jesus was crucified, even though it had seemed so to the disciples. God did not leave His Son in death (Ps. 16:8-11; Acts 2:25-36) but raised Him up and gave Him the victory. The times have been dark for us too, but God is not dead! He is *our* God, our Father, Creator of our earth and sky, ruler of our history from eternity to eternity, the living God who fills us with His joy and Spirit. Let the world and devils tremble before us; we shall not tremble before the world! We are storming the gates of hell, and its ramparts must fall before us (Matt. 16:18); for we bear the name and sonship, the glory and the keys, of Jesus Christ our Lord!

It is this that opens the whole world to us as the place and occasion for serving our Father and doing His will. We begin in the fellowship of the saints, where we uphold, trust, encourage, and love one another, rejoicing with the joys of a brother, weeping with him, raising those who fall, experiencing the benefits of God's gifts to the whole church as we add our gifts to those of others in the body of Christ. We have a greater hope to live by than the American dream, the land of opportunity, and the slogan "Get ahead." We are not that interested in "getting ahead." What the Lord wants us to have and use in the way of talents and blessings we will accept and cherish "as good stewards of God's varied grace" (1 Peter 4:10). But we are servants to one another. The highest man in the world's eyes is servant to the lowest, and the lowest to the highest, and both of them are kings. There is a kind of holy nakedness about us as we join in confessing our sins and receiving absolution in the name of our one Father, one Lord, and one Spirit. We pass nobody by. We make nobody inferior, unless it is ourselves in the freedom of our servanthood. The curse of covetousness is broken, the sin that, Paul confessed, deceived and slew him (Rom. 7:7-12) — the curse of pursuing our good and advantage. God is the Giver of all good gifts, and He will not cease to give. That is our freedom.

The love and joy of the church moves out also to the world, for we belong to its humanity, and it belongs to us. Now we find that we have an enormous advantage after all over our secular neighbor. For though we too find what we should do by knowing good and evil, we are not bound by such knowledge to protect ourselves or to measure our contribution by the rewards it may bring us in any degree whatsoever. The man who serves out of the knowledge of good and evil cannot really stop thinking of costs. He cannot help but ask, if he seems to be getting nowhere, whether the effort is worth it after all, whether his investment is getting a return. He cannot but be offended if nobody notices or says thank you.

This, then, is the point at which any love, however ardent at first, which is merely humanistic in its cry for the rescue of the inner city or for the deliverance of the Negro from oppression is bound to meet its great test. When the people who have gotten ahead do for the moment try to reach back to help those they have passed by, only to find their efforts costly, unrewarding, frustrating, and thankless, only to find also that the demands are insatiable, then backlash and retreat seem inevitable. Retreat will be supported and demanded above all by those who can now capitalize on this frustration to justify their own refusal to reach back in the first place. Mayors and councils, executives and legislators in state and nation can maintain an intensive zeal only so long. The time is coming, indeed it is already here, when excuses will be morally acceptable in the name of realism. Then the public conscience will be satisfied with tokens. The argument that "these people must do more to help themselves" will be very persuasive. The withdrawal will harden, silence will prevail, and society will forget.

But the church must not forget, and will not. The Lord has been dragging the church into an inescapable confrontation with the diseases of our culture. The church alone has the power to stick it out. As long as the heavenly Father says to us, "Do you hear this man cry?" the church will have to go. It doesn't matter whether the response to its attempted service is resentment or enmity, cynicism or suspicion, accusation or violence. The command "Love your enemies," hard as it is, can be fulfilled by the sons of the Father, who know what it means to be free of the need to flee the evil and pursue the good. They understand what the Scriptures mean when they speak of patience, long-suffering, not growing weary in well-doing, never flagging in zeal while serving the Lord (Rom. 12:9-21), not counting the frequency of forgiveness but forgiving seventy times seven (Matt. 18: 21-35). That is why the church can get more done toward helping people with less money than anybody else in the world. It has always been so!

And if this is folly to the world, it is a joyful folly to the man who knows God and thereby knows what life is all about. There is a strange splendor in St. Paul's many descriptions of the paradox of willing suffering. "We are fools for Christ's sake. . . . We are weak, but you are strong. You are held in honor, but we in disrepute. . . . We have become, and are now, as the refuse of the world, the off-scouring of all things." (1 Cor. 4:8-13)

We have much to thank God for and to be excited about in this business of serving. We also have lots to be forgiven for. Yet this God of ours is remarkable, and let's not underestimate Him. Remember the son who, when asked to serve in the vineyard, said, "I won't"? Somehow, by a curious unexplained force he found himself going anyhow

110

(Matt. 21:29)! That happens to Christians when they know the joy of repentance and of God's free Spirit.

The dawn is breaking for Christ's church again. We shall be seeing more and more of it! But we need to learn from our God how to comfort our people and set them free rather than harangue them. Only a hallelujah people who know how to rest in their God can do Him and the world what the collect calls "true and laudable service."

5

In the Deadness of Men —
The Word of Life (Witness)

This poem by Dona Hoffman, a Seattle housewife and mother of six, appeared on the back cover of *Advance* magazine, February 1967.

WITNESS

I sat in the pew,
and I listened to the silent anguish
of my brothers
being denounced for their failure to evangelize.

The sloped shoulder,
   the withdrawal,
      the burdened hearts
were mute beggary:
   Show us Jesus Christ
   and we will gladly share Him!
   We cannot share
   whom we do not know.

And after the damning
we were ushered out
to our busywork of choir rehearsals
   and bowling leagues
   and sewing circles.

When I first read that poem I wept. I found myself reading it again and again. "Show us Jesus Christ and we will gladly share Him! *We cannot share whom we do not know. And after the damning we were ushered out . . . ."* I wept because I sensed that Dona had put her finger on the greatest hunger of Christendom today, a hunger hidden beneath the surface of many troubles and one that we have hardly recognized. *"We cannot share whom we do not know."* The italics are hers.

Can you see how right she is? Have we *known* the Christ we know we ought to know? What do our orthodox and safely familiar doctrinal assertions mean to those who hear, and why should they touch the heart, and why should anybody believe or even be interested? These are fearful questions, as I know from experience. And I have no doubt that they have haunted many another conscientious preacher and thinking seminary student. Young men leave the seminaries as pastors and bring with them their Bibles and doctrines. They know the difference between the true and the false. But now, when they get into pulpits, what shall they say? Suddenly the old phrases seem so very trite. Even new illustrations seem trivial and artificial. What is the Gospel? What is its peace, joy, power, life? What is so exclusively and offensively "true" about it? I can understand why a young seminarian, failing to find answers that ring true to life in theology, would turn to other disciplines like psychology in the hope of finding what he seeks. I can understand the appeal of bold and radical frontier theologies, for they at least appear to be fresh, challenging, and even righteous in their judgments. They want to be meaningful and to address man as man is today; and men today, in their impatience with superficiality and meaninglessness, are ready to give them a hearing.

Let me use the term *liberal theology* in a broad sense

113

to cover every theology since Friedrich Schleiermacher (1768—1834), whose primary concern was to understand, maintain contact with, and address modern man. Schleiermacher and his successors recognized this, at least, that the world after the scientific revolution was a new and different world. Men no longer understood their world in ancient categories, whether Biblical or Aristotelian. The old language looked like myth and seemed more a barrier than a help to communication. So the liberal faced forward boldly, accepting the realities of a new age as he understood them and bringing with him as much of the old as he could make meaningful. In adopting this posture he faced grave theological hazards. His judgments were necessarily selective and subjective. His emphasis on the church's contact with and participation in the world readily led to a devaluation of the church's holiness and nonconformity.

Over against him stood the *conservative*. Let me risk another broad definition. Under the impact of a world that had changed, an irreverent and critical world that declared itself independent of God and treated religion as an antiquated superstition surviving out of sheer authoritarian stubbornness, the conservative was concerned to recover and preserve the essence and power of Christianity and to assert its holiness and differentness from the world. Conservative Lutheran Christians repudiated the rationalism of the 18th century, retreated to the best of 17th-century orthodoxy, reaffirmed the Lutheran Confessions and Luther, and insisted on the Scriptures alone as the source and norm of faith and life. Their problem, as the liberals saw it, was that they would not take seriously the revolution of human thought that characterized their age. Conservatives were accused of defending their people against the modern, of demanding that all religious thinking be done as though this were still the 17th or the 16th or even the 1st century.

German Lutheranism went through great torments in the 19th century. Some gained a long reprieve from the struggle by emigrating to the American frontier. But in the last decades the reprieve has ended. Perhaps the hand of God is still covering us in the cleft of the rock. We are not yet in a position to see the backside of God. In such a stress, however, Dona Hoffman's appeal is vital. What is the Gospel, and why should anyone today believe it? How are we to help the layman who, when we say "Evangelize! Witness!" answers us, "But what shall I say?" Now of course, we have dealt with that problem all along. We produce literature, question-and-answer sheets, suggestions for community visitations. And yet something is lacking. We use all the good words about the cross and blood, about guilt and forgiveness, about life and hope in the resurrection. Sometimes something gets through, especially when we are really guilty or when we are undergoing surgery or a loved one dies.

But what am I supposed to say to my satisfied neighbor? Shall I quote John 3:16, "God so loved the world that He gave His only Son"? All right, I'll try it. But I don't really have much confidence in it, for he'll think that's nice religious language, and I'll feel good I said it, and I'll hope that the Holy Spirit may manage to do something with it and that my concern and love came through. But really, why should he believe it? Why should it do something to him? Why is this message the hope of the world and of his own life? Why should "salvation," whatever that really is, be "good news" to him? Come to think of it, why should it be good news even to me?

Many pastors have felt a kind of hollowness and emptiness in their ministry, though they would surely find it hard to admit their feelings. Imagine a pastor going to a member like Dona and saying, "You hit me hard. I'd like to show you Jesus Christ, but I'm discovering that I don't know Him very well myself!" But pastors can't say that to their lay people! The layman expects pastors to *know!* What is the pastor for? Why did he go to the seminary? If he admits he doesn't know very much about the Gospel or how to use it to make people lighthearted in Christ Jesus so that when they leave the church they will be singing hallelujah all week long, he is impugning the seminary and the whole theological system. And what will the brethren think?

Thank God that in the Lord Jesus and by our baptism we are free from every curse and threat of failure, ignorance, and inadequacy—free to cry out to our Father in heaven! The promise stands, and we don't have to be scientific students of the Bible to understand it: "Ask, and it will be given you; seek, and you will find; knock, and it will be opened to you. For everyone [including even a troubled pastor] who asks receives, and he who seeks finds, and to him who knocks it will be opened." (Luke 11:9)

So let's not be afraid and ashamed of exposing ourselves in the inadequacies, fears, doubts, and follies that seem so dreadful. Let's be bold enough to quit bragging that we have had the Gospel all along, honest enough to quit accusing our drifting youth of unbelief. The truth may well be that they are starving for the bread of life, haven't really been fed, and are simply looking elsewhere for something to eat—something that will satisfy their craving to find themselves and be worth something. We know we have something precious. We respond to it, we experience joy and sing hallelujah and get a thrill of meaning out of our knowledge of God and our privilege of prayer. But to the people in the pew the church's message comes through as archaic and superficial, weighted with answers to questions they are not asking or don't understand, focusing on issues that get hung up in idle and speculative rationality and cannot reach the heart. It is impossible to compensate for the lack of comfort and freedom in preaching by urging the need for love, service, evangelism, and stewardship. The reaction then is sure to be just as depressing as Dona's poem. "I listened to the silent anguish of my brothers being denounced for their failure to evangelize. . . . And after the damning we were ushered out." What a way to go!

I suggest that we who are pastors have Dona's poem made into a plaque and mount it on the wall of our sacristy or study for a year or two, perhaps right next to Luther's Sacristy Prayer. And let us all pledge that we shall let it torment us and purge us from our fear of confessing how little we know, how little we understand.

And let us pray daily according to the promise, "Seek, and you will find." And let us begin to agonize over our sermon texts as we have too seldom done, taking them apart word for word, asking continually in our wrestling with God: "Why should this mean anything? Why did it get people excited when it was written? Why is it said this way, and not the way I would have wished, in view of my dogmatic tradition? Why doesn't it hang together? What is good about the good news contained here? How can I translate this and make it lift up the hearts of Christ's holy people? How can it be used to make them sigh with the relief of a burden lifted? How can it exalt the valleys of the depressed and bring down the mountains of the proud? For, God help me, there is one thing this sermon must do, whatever else it may do—it must send my people home resting in quiet again in their God like a child on its mother's breast, and with a divine hallelujah on their lips!"

Not until the Lord blesses us with at least the beginning of an answer to such questions will we start worrying about outlines and rhetorical techniques. And if we find that it takes 20 hours a week out of our busy schedules to do this, let it take 20 hours. The job of the preacher is to let God speak to him out of His Book—not to run around doing a thousand good things, but to devote himself "to prayer and to the ministry of the Word," as Acts 6:4 says.

For the Word of God alone is the hammer that breaks the rock in pieces (Jer. 23:29). The Word of God alone comes down like rain and snow and carries the promise of accomplishing the purpose for which God sent it (Is. 55:10-11). The Word of God alone has power to penetrate the joints and marrow of human defenses more sharply than any two-edged sword (Heb. 4:12). The Word of God alone is the seed that is sown, and only when it is sown does it have the power either to be hated and rejected or to bring forth fruit (Matt. 13:1-23).

We may be grateful to liberal theologians for demanding so insistently that we take seriously the world as it is and not pretend we can find safety by living as though nothing had happened since the 17th century. But we can and must challenge liberal thought for its superficial and prejudicial use of the Scriptures, for its readiness to write off any Biblical idea that does not carry the proper appeal to modern man, without first pressing the question what that strange history or form of language had to say in its original context.

For example, it is cheap and easy to join in the cry that since modern man doesn't think of a "God out there," the only God we must think of is the God in here, that is, the God in everything, a pantheistic deity.

It is cheap and easy to say that since modern man has no vision of God and cannot comprehend God-talk, God is dead.

It is cheap and easy to diagnose modern man out of the perspectives of psychology and to argue that what was once seen as universal depravity is only a social illness.

118

It is cheap and easy to notice that the world is getting smaller, that the distinctiveness of Christianity is more and more difficult to maintain, and thereupon to lift out of the Bible the theme of the cosmic Christ who is Lord and Savior of all nations and active in everything that is good — and to call that Christianity.

It is cheap and easy to equate God's grace in creation with His grace in redemption — as though this were not a fallen world.

It is cheap and easy to say that wherever healing occurs, whether by a witch doctor or in a modern hospital or on a psychiatrist's couch, it is a manifestation of Christ and His universal and saving love.

It is cheap and easy to conform to the relativism of our world, to glory in relativism as though man had nothing to cling to except his own daring act of personal faith and decision.

It is cheap and easy to turn all law and ethics into relativism, to find the countless hard cases which prove that there are no absolutes and that man can finally depend only on himself.

It is cheap and easy to promote activism and love as a "Gospel," as though Christ's Gospel can be conveyed without words as well as with them.

The theological issue that seems to underlie the whole of the liberal outlook today seems to me to be the failure to recognize what evil really is in the profound Biblical sense. For there are two ways to approach the question, "What is evil?" One is to stand within and under the knowledge of good and evil and then to make distinctions on the basis of what seems obvious to the open eye (Gen. 3:5). This approach is characteristic of liberal thought and theology as it summons men to arms in the battle against evil. Thus human privation, suffering, and oppression are seen to be evil. Inequity and injustice are evil. War is evil. Intolerance and provincialism are evil, especially in religion (hence the text "No man comes to the Father but by Me" [John 14:6] is made to say, "Everybody comes to the Father by Me"). Legalism and moral absolutism are evil. The church serves God and fulfils its calling, therefore, when it detects, hates, and resists evil and loves and promotes the contrary good. Good men are those who labor with the good God for the suppression of the evil and the attainment of the good. That is one way to interpret good and evil, and within its province it is not without validity.

The other way, however, is to stand above man's alleged capacity to know good and evil, and to recognize that the root of all evil is nothing else than man's willingness to assume that he *really knows* what is good and what is evil, what is advantageous and what is disadvantageous for him and for humanity. For that is his idolatry. That is the point at which he usurps the place of God and then blasphemes God by attempting to harness Him to his own vision, understanding, and purpose. It is difficult to see this, for the distinctions we make between good and evil seem to accord so obviously with common sense, love, and godly piety. Jesus showed the difficulty when He thanked His Father for having "hidden these things from the wise and understanding and revealed them to babes" (Matt. 11:25-26). "Yea, Father, for such was Thy gracious will," He added. The wisdom of God clashes here with the wisdom of man, but God's must prevail, for He is "Lord of heaven and earth."

St. Paul learned it, he confesses in a fascinating bit of autobiography in Rom. 7, when the commandment "You shall not covet" finally broke through to him. Coveteousness, as we saw in our first chapter, is the sin of having one's eyes open (Gen. 3:5; "the lust of the eyes," 1 John 2:16),

120

judging something we see to be good and desirable, and directing our life toward having it. Its converse is to see and judge something to be evil and repulsive and to direct our life toward avoiding it. Now what is harmful or immoral about that? Surely it does not seem immoral to want a thing, as long as we do not violate our neighbor's rights in the process of getting it!

Yet this little commandment turned out to be the hammerlike Word of God that broke the rock in pieces. It vitiated all the obedience Saul of Tarsus and his fellow Pharisees had boasted of before God. Suddenly wherever Saul looked in his life, above all in his religious zeal and persecution of the church, he saw nothing but pursuit and defense of advantages, nothing but a lusting after what he by his wisdom judged to be the "good" and a hatred of what he had decided was "evil." This was covetousness, identified in Eph. 5:5 as idolatry. Saul resisted for a while, like an ox kicking against the goads of its driver (Acts 26:14). But when he got near Damascus, he broke down. The light from heaven blinded him, closed his eyes to the covetous wisdom of man, in order that he might see the face of Jesus Christ (2 Cor. 4:6) and hear His voice. Thus Saul had to give up his pride and career in the Law, and all the advantages of Judaism (Phil. 3:2-11). Like any worthless and guilty harlot, tax collector, or Gentile, he had to be baptized into the name of Jesus. Only so could he now belong to God and God's people. He had to put on Christ, the wedding garment of the Kingdom (Gal. 3:27; Matt. 22:11-13). The scales fell from his eyes, and he could see what he had never been able to see before. "Blessed are the pure in heart, for they shall see God" (Matt. 5:8). That is, blessed are those who give up pretending that they are seeking God when in reality they are seeking only what they have decided is good.

To give up the knowledge of good and evil for the

knowledge of God, that is the new wisdom. Those who possess it look out on the world with a cheerful pessimism — cheerful because there is an answer and they live by it; pessimism because there is only one answer, and the world hates it. Ecclesiastes tells the story of the cheerful pessimist. The "Preacher" knows all the wrong answers and how deadly and empty they are. As he lives himself experimentally into one after another of the possibilities of the good life, he can only conclude that "all is vanity and a striving after wind." "So I hated life," he says (2:17). Strange that a man who can have his way in any direction he wants to go should hate life. Strange, but how very real! I have talked to many students who knew just what that means. Everything lies before you, but you don't know where to go, and you hate life for confronting you with so terrifying a paralysis! You hate life for not defining itself! And in hating life, you hate God! Yet the Preacher of Ecclesiastes is cheerful. He knows and fears God. Therefore each day God gives is a great joy to him. He serves God, accepts even pain from God, and lets God judge what is good and what is evil. (Eccl. 12:13-14)

So we Christians too are cheerful pessimists. We do not believe in the goodness of the world or of men, or in an evolutionlike process ever upward. We place no ultimate confidence in human wisdom. Oh yes, there are times when the evidence conspires to make us wonder. We see the prosperity and stability of our secular, worldly neighbors. They are lovely people, and we hate to judge their motives. We find ourselves thinking about them almost the way Old Testament psalmists did about the so-called wicked, meaning not so much the morally reprehensible as simply outsiders from the community of promise (for example, Ps. 37; 49; 73; 94; Job 21; 27). In many cases the predatory aggressiveness ascribed to such "wicked" suggests that pagan invaders may be in view. The wicked succeed so well, and God's people do so poorly by contrast! You wonder what value religion may have after all! Yet always the verdict is impending judgment. Success is brief and illusory, and man is not measured by his passing pomp. The richest of men are like the beasts that perish (Ps. 49). The look of solidity is illusory. That prosperous neighbor is what the successful princes and landowners of Judah and Israel were, when the prophets accused them as oppressors for having passed by the poor on their way up and for claiming their status as a right. Ecclesiastes describes their dignity and security as vanity and wind. "Great was the fall of it" (Matt. 7:27). Hope and promise lie solely in the Word of God. To hear that Word and live by it is to build upon the Rock.

We entertain no illusions, therefore, about the nature and destiny of this fallen world or about the ultimate outcome of all the works of man. To compromise this judgment in any way is to cheapen, dilute, and destroy the very polarity over against which the alternative of the Gospel becomes meaningful, and thus to turn the Gospel into a hollow shell.

We know about evil. But now, before I carry this argument further, it is necessary to recognize that there is indeed a certain theological validity in the view I ascribed to liberalism, which distinguishes good from evil from within and under such knowledge. There is no question but that Biblical theology does this very thing too. Here we must take note of two approaches to the problem of evil that appear in the Scriptures alongside (though in a sense also under) the "knowledge of good and evil" theology. For the people of God are quite aware that evil is real. They do see and know evil. They do not deny pain or pretend it doesn't hurt or dismiss it as an illusion. Suffering is terribly real. The question is, "Why does it happen?" Especially, "Why does it happen to the people of God, who live by the promises?" Two kinds of answers to that question predominate, and both are theologically important, also for our preaching of the Gospel.

The first is that suffering and pain come to man as retribution for sin. Thus suffering preaches the Law. That is exactly the point of Gen. 3 and its curses. The divine irony comes through. "You grabbed for the good, did you? You thought you could be god, did you? Well then, as you leave the Garden take this baggage along with you — pain, weeds, sweat, frustration, domination of one by the other, and above all, dirt! Walk in the dirt when you till the ground, and know with every step that dirt is what you are and to dirt you shall return!" That's a powerful word, and we have no business weakening it or compromising it as though it isn't true anymore. It isn't true *for us,* because this accusation of dirt and pain, valid as it is, no longer has any power to separate us from the love of God which is in Jesus Christ our Lord (Rom. 8:31-38), who was made a curse for us (Gal. 3:13). It isn't true for us, because we as children of God now participate willingly in all the consequences of the Fall. By faith in the promises of God we do not attempt to escape the humanity to which we still belong. But that is the only way in which that word of fearful retribution ceases to be true in the full power of its ironic curse.

It is remarkable how well the world of the knowledge of good and evil understands this principle of retribution! "What did I do to deserve this?" men ask. "There is no justice," they complain. Yet by their very anger they acknowledge that the message of retribution is getting through. We need to capitalize on this sort of thing, not weaken it. Suffering shouts the message that the sufferer is not worth very much, and people who look in on the sufferer from the outside tend to concur in the accusation. Read the tremendous passage in which Job takes up this point (Job 29 — 30)!

When he was rich and clean and had everything going for him, everybody bowed to him and listened and thought he was the wisest of men. But now that he is beaten down, poor, in pain and rags, nobody is interested in his wisdom anymore. They don't even hear him when he is talking. All they care about is giving him advice.

It's really funny, but it is so true. We judge by appearances, we are respecters of persons. The measure of importance is the dignity, poise, clothes, house, office, furnishings, wit, and the rest of it in which a man frames his self-portrait. Thus man concurs in the verdict that suffering and prosperity come as retribution. A man who looks like a bum must be worthless. A man who looks like a million must be important. Things are as they appear to be. How God laughs at us! Yet notice that in both cases "evil" has the last word. The rich man dies. Lazarus dies. The size of their respective funerals and tombstones doesn't matter to the worms, who enjoy both equally. (Luke 16:22)

The second kind of answer to the question, "Why does evil happen?" is the theme that evil is demonic, that it afflicts God's people from the outside, that is, from devils and ungodly men. But God steps in, or will step in, to deliver His people, and their deliverance will come by way of the destruction of their enemies. This point of view is suggested already in the Exodus history, where the deliverance of Israel comes by way of the destruction of the Egyptian army in the Red Sea. The people exult: "I will sing unto the LORD, for He has triumphed gloriously; the horse and his rider He has thrown into the sea. The LORD is my Strength and my Song, and He has become my Salvation" (Ex. 15). Read the rest of it. There is not a hint of pity for the Egyptian soldiers whose bodies have washed ashore. This approach to evil is characteristic of the so-called imprecatory psalms (for example, Ps. 109). The prayer for the salvation of God's people and for the destruction of the enemy is one piece, two sides of the same coin, without a thought of pity for the oppressor. We must take such cries seriously for what they were — cries for salvation, for deliverance from evil and the power of darkness in which the only thing to be seen was the tyranny the enemy was exerting on the child or people of God.

Again, the theme occurs in Dan. 7, where the nations that have overflowed Judah in successive waves of oppression are pictured as predatory beasts arising from the sea. Their end is coming, however, on the day when God gives the Kingdom and all dominion to "one like a son of man" (Dan. 7:13-14), that is, to Israel, God's people (Dan. 7:18, 22, 27). Here again, deliverance implies the breaking of the power of the enemy. In the Gospels the evil that men suffer is sometimes portrayed as demonic. People are made fit for the Kingdom when the devils that possess them are cast out (Matt. 12:28). Salvation comes by the destruction of the foe and the abolition of all evil.

Now this too is a familiar and precious theme for the proclamation of the Gospel. The Lord does not hide the terror and threats of devils and men from us but only invites us not to be afraid. Name the force that threatens you (there are lists in Rom. 8:35-39; Col. 2:8-23). Whatever it may be, Jesus in His death and resurrection has gained the victory! He reigns in triumph as the Son of Man, to whom all the kingdoms and glory have been given (Dan. 7:13-14; Ps. 110:1). Satan is bound, and even if he is loosed for a time, he can no longer tyrannize the saints of God. (Rev. 20)

Thus the reality of suffering is not denied. Evil as men experience and fear it from within their "knowledge of good and evil" is no illusion. No reckoning with the problem of evil in the Bible is adequate that fails to give full voice to the two themes we have just reviewed, retribution and the demonic. Both of these distinguish clearly between prosperity and adversity. Both, in fact, accept and build on the distinction as men make it from within their natural wisdom and ordinary experience.

There is much here, therefore, to commend the liberal view that the task of the church is to detect and combat every force of evil and oppression under which men today are bound, and thus to manifest the saving hand of God. Yet a problem remains. Part of the problem is that the ill-defined but aggressively sentimental piety of contemporary Protestantism fails to deal seriously with the nature of evil even on the level of retribution or the demonic. The demonic element in human oppression is not taken with full seriousness, for that would imply that men are helpless and captive under forces they can neither understand nor control, like the Israelites in Egypt or the devil-possessed in Jesus' day. But this would make the salvation of men depend on a miraculous intervention of God, the argument goes, thus denying to men and the church both freedom and responsibility. Thus a world view that magnifies the moral responsibility and rational capacity of man to diagnose and cure all his ills has not much use for the devil or for God, except perhaps as symbols of what men think and do.

But retribution is not taken seriously either, for this would seem to conflict with the notion of God's universal love. Surely God does not desire evil for men, but only good! God's saving hand is evident, therefore, whenever an evil is overcome or a disability healed. What then is the source of the evil? There seems to be little interest in facing that question on the theological level. The natural diagnosis is all that matters. Evil is the product of bad engineering or of drinking before driving. Evil is the effect of natural catastrophes which men are not yet able to prevent or control. Evil is the force that causes physical illness or disability.

Evil is the product of political, economic, psychological, or sociological pressures. Evil may even be the effect of some undefined baser and lower nature in man.

Anyone who meets the problem of evil on such levels and helps overcome it is an instrument of God's "salvation." In His attack on evil God uses the church, but He also uses any other positive social force that labors to set man free, to integrate him into total personhood in relation to himself and to society. God is good. He is the force of healing, wherever this is found. When a man has experienced the good and has found healing and wholeness, he has somehow encountered God. But it is primitive and outmoded to imagine that the evil men experience expresses the judgment and wrath of God (retribution); or that evil is demonic, holding men helplessly captive and dooming them to death. Since the opened eye of man cannot "see" such a theological dimension to the question of evil, man in his wisdom judges such elements of Biblical theology to be meaningless, archaic, and illusory.

Such a theology appears wise, generous, zealous, and loving. In reality, however, it is one-sided and sub-Christian. Only an arbitrary, self-determined, and prejudiced optimism can claim to detect God's goodness in the experience of healing yet refuse to see God's wrath in the contrary experience of suffering and death. Furthermore, a salvation that consists merely in offering limited and temporary relief of particular pains fails utterly to get at the vital problem of man—his rebellion against and ignorance of God. If the lost son finds himself in desperate want after running away from home and wasting his inheritance, it may indeed be an act of mercy to him to offer him a job tending swine (Luke 15:15), but this can hardly be called his "salvation." To drink water from Jacob's well is refreshing indeed, but he who drinks this water will surely thirst again (John 4:13). Those who ate manna in the wilderness, or even the loaves that fed 5,000 men, still died (John 6:49, 58). Daily bread is indeed a great gift of divine mercy, which the Father pours out with sun and rain on all men, whether they know and honor Him or not (Matt. 5:45). God does indeed manifest His mercy on a lost world when He grants prosperity even to the ungodly, heals broken bodies, forces society to work for a semblance of justice and to relieve social inequities, or answers the prayer of a nation for an end to war. But such mercy does not yet turn sinners into sons or set them free of the knowledge of good and evil so that they may know God. It does not reveal the holiness of God or create a holy people.

Liberal theology is deficient, therefore, in its grasp of the fundamental problem of man from the Biblical perspective, as well as in its understanding of the nature and action of God. On the one hand, it cannot deal seriously with the themes of retribution and the demonic, which presuppose fallen man's distinction between good and evil. But even worse (and this is my final point), liberal theology seems incapable of knowing the God who *condemns man's very attempt to know good and evil as the basic idolatry!*

For the true knowledge of God is reserved to little children, as we have seen, to children who "have no knowledge of good and evil" (Deut. 1:39). We become such children when we learn to confess that we don't really know how to judge and decide between what is advantageous or disadvantageous for ourselves or for our world. It is enough for us that our God possesses the fullness of such knowledge. We therefore walk with our heavenly Father in the simplicity of faith—hearing, serving, and obeying Him without calculation and without fear.

Thus we live by a wisdom *above* the wisdom of fallen man. At this level of faith the distinctions we make *under* and within the old wisdom no longer apply. *Under* the knowledge of good and evil we may indeed take note of many forces of violence and oppression that heap evils upon men, and label these *demonic*. Given the world of fallen man as it is and the necessity that even Christians continue to live in it, such a perspective must belong to and remain a part of Christian theology, as we have said. But we are not talking about that now. In the higher kingdom in which we now stand, only God knows what is good and what is evil for us, and we gladly surrender such distinctions to Him.

Again, *under* the knowledge of good and evil we experience grief and tragedy, label such experiences "evil," and perhaps recognize in them an aspect of divine judgment and *retribution*. This perspective too is a necessary and valid element in Christian theology. But when we stand in that higher wisdom in which we no longer trust our eyes to tell us what is good or evil, or dark or light, or bitter or sweet (Is. 5:20), the only thing that matters is the wisdom, Word, and promise of our heavenly Father. At this point even the language and problematics of retribution are left behind.

What is important now is the purity of heart by which we "see God" (Matt. 5:8) when we no longer attempt to judge or contradict Him on the basis of evidences that seem so persuasive to us. What is important now is that the "angels" of God's little children (we are such children) "always behold the face of their Father who is in heaven" (Matt. 18:10) and have no time left to calculate the fearful things or the attractive things that seem to be so real on earth. What is important now is to know the things the Father has chosen to hide from the wise and understanding and reveal only to babes (Matt. 11:25). What matters now is the privilege we have of addressing our Father in heaven not on sophisticated man-to-man terms but with a little child's "Papa" or "Daddy," with the "Abba" of the little child in the world of Jesus' day (Mark 14:36; Rom. 8:15-16; Gal. 4:6). For we are not merely *children* of God. We are *very little* children. But a little child does not know or understand very much. He is satisfied not to know. He surrenders the fearful questions and finds quiet in simply lying at his mother's breast (Ps. 131). It is enough for him to know that his Shepherd leads him and walks with him. That is why he can walk even through the valley of the shadow of death and fear no evil. (Ps. 23)

Here, I think, lies the greatest failure of liberal theology. In its determination to be aggressive and wise and mature, liberal theology presumes to know too much. Its categories of thought presuppose and consistently assume that man knows good and evil and can base his strategy and actions on that knowledge. Liberal theology does not understand how to be a little child. Hence it fashions God in the image of its own intensive moral concern and piety. It fancies itself capable of interpreting to the world what God must have in mind – as though man could really comprehend what God wants and approves, or resists and disapproves. Thereby it becomes a blind leader of the blind. Because it takes pride in its adulthood, it cannot enter the kingdom of heaven. (Matt. 18:3)

All of this is comprehensible, however, only to those who "turn and become like little children." Only a child can comprehend the "foolishness of God," which is "wiser than men" (1 Cor. 1:25). The LORD God exposes and defies the natural wisdom of man. He hurls into the face of human reason and judgment one text after another that proclaims that He alone is God (monotheism). God will not tolerate the efforts of men to subsume Him under their knowledge of good and evil. Against any attempt to limit Him, the one God insists that He is the doer of *everything* that is done – not only of things men approve as "good" but also of things they abhor and in righteous indignation label as "evil."

If a man protests, "Surely, the good God cannot be like that!" the God of the Bible replies, "Oh, can't I?" And then He credits Himself boldly with actions that men regard as immoral and unworthy of Him, that polytheistic and dualistic religions would ascribe to evil deities and devils, that men today prefer to attribute to unfortunate "chance," or that seem quite obviously to have their cause in the lusts of men and the corruption of society. The one God declares that He does not only the "good" things but the "evil" things as well!

We must examine a number of such texts. Let Deut. 32:39 speak first, as a paradigm for them all:

> See now that I, even I am He,
>   and now there is no god beside Me;
> I kill and I make alive;
>   I wound and I heal;
>   and there is none that can deliver out of My hand.

Our natural piety resists a text like that. We hasten to reinterpret it, modify it, cloud it, remove its sting. Surely the God who commands us not to kill does not kill! Better to say He simply "allows" deaths and wounds to happen, or that He permits the sin of man to express itself to its full consequences, or that He grants men freedom even if this entails the risk of its irresponsible violation, or that He perhaps does some of the killing but not all of it! We say such things because our natural notions of justice and morality simply cannot comprehend a God who says, "I kill!" But God accepts none of our modifications and evasions. He is out to destroy the natural wisdom by which we imagine we can judge Him. He is determined that we shall not be God, that we shall either give up trying to be wise and like God or else perish in our wisdom. For He alone is God!

Therefore He insists: "I kill and I make alive; I wound and I heal; and there is none that can deliver out of My hand!" Do you want your God as the God who heals and makes alive? Then you must have Him also as the God who does the wounding and the killing. You cannot have *no* God, as though "good and evil" as you experience them have only natural causes. You cannot have *two* gods, one who does the bad things and another who does the good. Human responsibility and guilt and natural causes are in no way to be denied. But over and above and in them, whether in death or in life, whether in suffering or in deliverance, the *one* God is in action. God does it all! "I am He, and there is no god beside Me!"

Dare we translate such a word of God into our own times? "I, your God, create your wars, the bloody slaughter of men by men, the lists of the dead and wounded, the destruction and the waste, the overpowering tragedy that tears at the heart of families and nations." Can you believe and trust a God like that?

Try Him again. "Do you see the growth of crime, the vandalism and robbery, the sadistic murders done for the sheer enjoyment of a moment of power? Do you shudder at it and fear it?" says your God. "Then know that these deaths too are from Me. I don't cause only the sweet and gentle deaths of the aged and infirm. I cause the deaths you abhor, the deaths of the young and innocent, the tragic and unjust deaths, the arbitrary and senseless deaths, the deaths by manslaughter and assassination. I don't do only the things you call good and nice! I do the things you call terrible! 'And there is none that can deliver out of My hand.' " What will you do with a God like that? Hate Him? Rule Him out of existence? Or flee like a child into His arms, knowing that no other God exists who can deliver us from evil?

Or again: "I don't create only the healthy cells in the bodies of men; I create also the cancers! Not only the seeing eyes and hearing ears are Mine, but also eyes that do not see, ears that cannot hear, tongues that cannot speak, minds that cannot fully function." (Ex. 4:11)

Or again, hear God say: "Do you want Me to heal your rotten society? Then know Me first as the God who creates and confronts you with every symptom of that rottenness. The crowded slums are My doing, the rats are from Me. I create the rotted steps and the falling plaster, the riots and the burning, the bitterness of race against race and class against class, the fear and frustration and despair. It is all from Me!" What will you do with a God like that?

And still again: "Do you want Me to raise the church from its coma, to heal its confusions and divisions and agony, to satisfy its hungers, and to fill it with peace and purpose and power? Then know first that it is I who struck her down and set enemies against her and heaped confusion and division upon her and exposed her as helpless and fearful before the world. Let that be the beginning of your comfort, that you know that I have done it. The darkness is from Me! 'I wound and I heal; and there is none that can deliver out of My hand.'"

Still we protest. "Surely, God," we say, "this isn't really You! I cannot believe that You would do some of the things You say You do. Surely the evils of the slums, the oppressions of the poor, the crimes and murders, the predatory aggressions of man against man—surely these are our doing and not Yours! For if You credit Yourself with the evils men afflict on one another, will they not despise You, consider themselves blameless, and become the more irresponsible?"

And God will reply: "You must understand what I am saying and what I am not saying. The ungodliness of man is man's alone, not Mine. The wisdom men trust, their pride and confidence that they know good and evil, their determination to live by the sight of their own eyes rather than by My Word, their passionate pursuit of whatever delights them and their terrified flight from whatever threatens them—that is their own doing. That is what blocks their ears and hardens their hearts against Me. That is the absolute evil, the 'original sin,' the secret slavery that seduces the heart and life of every man. Out of that evil come all the oppressions and violence of a man against his brother, the evil thoughts, murder, adultery, fornication, theft, false witness, slander. (Matt. 15:19)

"But now know one thing more," God says. " 'I will destroy the wisdom of the wise, and the cleverness of the clever I will thwart' (1 Cor. 1:19; Is. 29:14). The clay is not allowed to judge and fault the potter. The thing formed shall not say of him who formed it, 'He has no understanding' (Is. 29:16). For I am God alone. If a man boasts of his wisdom, he shall be a fool. If he boasts that he is free, he shall be a slave. If he boasts that he is responsible, I shall lay burdens on him till they utterly crush him. If he imagines he can save the world, he shall be found only to add to its destruction. If he boasts of his strength, he shall be weak. If he boasts of the life he has created, I shall return him to the dirt from which he came. For men must learn that 'I, even I am He, and there is no god beside Me. I kill and I make alive; I wound and I heal; and there is none that can deliver out of My hand.' "

Is that really so hard, so foolish? Can we not surrender our wisdom before such a God and become little children again, resting in quiet on our mother's breast (Ps. 131)? Must we comprehend God and integrate and make sense out of Him through our categories of understanding? Is it not enough to be able to pray, "Abba, Father, Thy will be done on earth as it is in heaven"? Or to hear our God say, "Be still and know that I am God" (Ps. 46:10)? Or, "I kill *and I make alive; I wound and I heal*"?

That is what God is finally after, throughout this Bible of ours. "If anyone among you thinks that he is wise in this age, let him become a fool that he may become wise" (1 Cor. 3:18). If it kills us to give up our wisdom, it is God who does the killing so that He can make us truly alive. God wants repentance of the sort He pleads for in the prophet Hosea, when He invites Israel to turn to Him in their utter distress and to say:

> Come, let us return to the LORD;
>> for He has torn, that He may heal us;
>> He has stricken, and He will bind us up.
> After two days He will revive us;
>> on the third day He will raise us up,
>> that we may live before Him.
> Let us know, let us press on to know the LORD;
>> His going forth is sure as the dawn;
>> He will come to us as the showers,
>> as the spring rains that water the earth.
>> (Hos. 6:1-3)

Hannah understood this too.

> There is none holy like the LORD,
>> there is none besides Thee;
>> there is no rock like our God. . . .
> The LORD kills and brings to life;
>> He brings down to Sheol and raises up.
> The LORD makes poor and makes rich;
>> He brings low, He also exalts.
>> (1 Sam. 2:2, 6-7)

Recall her story, the burden of barrenness she bore for so long. It was an "evil," and she had wept much over it. Yet

136

it never occurred to her to attribute her barrenness to some *devil,* or even to wonder what possible *retribution* the Lord might be inflicting on her. "Natural causes" are not in the picture either. "The LORD had closed her womb" (1 Sam. 1:5-6). It was also the LORD who answered her prayer and gave her a son (1 Sam. 1:9-28). That is monotheism, and the whole answer. "There is none besides Thee," Hannah sings. "The LORD brings low, He also exalts."

In the story of Joseph the "evil" is done to him by his jealous brothers. Yet when the event has unfolded to its end, the important thing to Joseph is not that *they* did it but that *his God* did it. They intended evil, but God intended good (Gen. 50:20). It is easy enough to see that now, in retrospect. It was not easy to see it in those dark and fearful years of slavery and imprisonment. Yet even in that darkness Joseph's comfort and his capacity to love and forgive his brothers lay in the childlike faith of monotheism. It was finally God, not his brothers, who brought him low. It was God, therefore, who would also deliver and exalt him.

When Job had experienced the loss of all his children and property and when loathsome and painful boils covered him from head to foot, his wife urged him to "curse God and die" (Job 2:9). She spoke out of her knowledge of good and evil, judging that a God who would inflict such evils on Job is not worthy to be God. Job responded by calling her "one of the foolish women" (his term, perhaps, for a theological liberal). As for himself, Job would not attribute the "evil" to the Sabean invaders or to demonic forces like Satan. Nor did he raise the issue of retribution by searching out a possible cause within himself so as to be able to vindicate the "justice" of God. His reply was simply: "Shall we receive good at the hand of God, and shall we not receive evil?" (Job 2:10). The text adds the comment: "In all this Job did not sin with his lips." He was a monotheist, a little child who trusted his God and would not attempt to invoke any "knowledge of good and evil" against and in judgment on God or in a vain effort to comprehend God. God had done the killing and the wounding. God would also make alive and heal. And that, says the story, is what happened. (Job 42)

When the LORD's anger was kindled against David for numbering the people, the prophet Gad offered the choice of three punishments. David elected 3 days of pestilence, saying, "I am in great distress; let us fall into the hand of the LORD, for His mercy is great; but let me not fall into the hand of man" (2 Sam. 24:14). It is better to receive the "evil" from the God who not only kills but also in mercy makes alive again, than from conquering enemies who know only how to kill. Thus David walks directly into the judgment of God, into what all human experience knows only as "evil." Yet by that very act he takes refuge in God's mercy. Isn't that beautiful? That is monotheism. It is the faith of a little child.

When the Assyrian and later the Babylonian invaders swept down on Palestine like predatory beasts, devouring one petty kingdom after another, the prophets make it clear that they do not come by their own design, even though they may think so. It is the LORD who has sent them (Is. 10:5-7)! The LORD God of Israel brings the curse. He even takes the side of the conqueror against His own city and temple, against the covenant kings of David's line, against His own land and people! There is no full agreement on *why* this happens. The prophets Jeremiah and Ezekiel speak of retribution, ascribing the great evil to the enormity of Judah's sin. Ethan the Ezrahite, composer of Ps. 89, finds the wrath altogether inexplicable. The Book of Lamentations takes note of the sins of Jerusalem's prophets and priests (4:13) but concentrates for the most part on the apparent contradiction of Israel's hope and expectation. Habakkuk is tormented with the question, "Why?" Yet he leaves it unanswered and summons the people only to wait in faith and hope. Yet at one point there is unanimity. It is the LORD who has done it! God is the source of the "evil" that afflicts and destroys His people. And there is agreement also on another point, that the very God who afflicts Judah and Jerusalem so dreadfully is the only ground of their hope for the future! Once again we catch the force of monotheism! One God does it all, and though men may not understand Him, they are not to judge Him. "The LORD is in His holy temple; let all the earth keep silence before Him," says Habakkuk (2:20), and again: "In wrath remember mercy." (3:2)

What God is after, finally, is sons who will be little children. Only as little children will they know how to love and trust, serve and obey Him alone, and fear Him rather than what their wide-eyed wisdom judges to be "evil." The beauty of Jesus Christ is that He was just such a child! "Abba, Father," we hear Him pray, "all things are possible to Thee; remove this cup from Me; yet not what I will, but what Thou wilt" (Mark 14:36). The "evil" of the cross is painfully visible to Jesus. He knows its torment, shame, and death. He is aware of the demonic dimensions of the threat that lies against Him (Luke 22:3, 31, 53). He knows well enough that He is the victim of the conspiracy of men who have hardened their hearts against repentance and are plotting to kill Him in order to save themselves. He knows the intrigue at work among His own disciples — not only the conspiracy of Judas but also the false hope others invest in swords. Everything we call "evil" in terms of suffering, injustice, and human ungodliness surrounds Him.

Yet in Gethsemane none of this is in the picture! "Not what I will, but what Thou wilt," He prays. The only thing that matters is the will of His Father. The will and the work of God oppose the deathly sorrow of His soul (Mark 14:34). The "cup" He must drink comes not from devils, not from men, but from His Father. The very same God who gave Him life and declared Him to be "My beloved Son" (Matt. 3:17) now sends Him into death! And Jesus will have it so! He is a monotheist. He has said so explicitly in rejecting Satan's suggestions of compromise: "For it is written, 'You shall worship the Lord your God, and Him only shall you serve' " (Matt. 4:10). The Son, who knows His heavenly Father, "cannot serve two masters" (Matt. 6:24). Hence in His final crisis Jesus will not inject fallen man's "knowledge of good and evil" between His Father's command and His own response. He trusts the God who kills Him, for that same God also will make Him alive (Deut. 32:39). The confession of the church that "He was raised on the third day in accordance with the Scriptures" (1 Cor. 15:4) suggests how important the word of divine promise we have quoted from Hos. 6:1-2 was to Jesus personally. It was as though He heard His Father declaring it just to Him: "If I strike You down, My Son, I shall also bind You up. After two days I shall revive You; on the third day I shall raise You up, that You may live before Me." Thus Jesus walks to the cross like a little child, into the valley of the shadow of death, refusing to fear the evil, fearing and loving and trusting His Father only. That is His obedience, His righteousness, His victory!

Peter understood it on Pentecost day. "This Jesus, delivered up according to the definite plan and foreknowledge of God, you crucified and killed by the hands of lawless men. But God raised Him up!" (Acts 2:23-24). The one God both delivered Him up and raised Him up! The human plotters and crucifiers are not thereby excused. They are called to repentance. Yet because God planned and did it, their repentance is framed in the promise of forgiveness and life in the Spirit, through baptism into the name of Jesus Christ. (Acts 2:38)

140

Thus God overthrows our knowledge of good and evil. The cross is horrible by all standards of human sight and judgment, yet God demands of us that we call it blessed. The Friday on which Jesus was crucified saw the evil of man at its worst, yet God demands that we call that day "Good." No meal can possibly be more repulsive and gory in conception and language and reality than that of the body crucified and the blood shed on the unholy hill of the skull. Yet God demands that we *eat* it and declares that precisely in this offensive eating we shall have life (John 6:53) and forgiveness of sins (Matt. 26:28). And now our risen Lord summons us to be little children as He was a little child, to follow Him, to bear the cross, to lose our lives for His sake, to fear no evil, and finally to rise from the dead and be glorified with Him.

Any man who still insists on being wise, however, must finally know his folly. The good he grasps for will elude him, and the evil he flees will get him. For God declares in His wrath: "I will not allow you to harness Me as your ally in your idolatrous pursuit of what you think is good and in your flight from what you fear is evil. I do the killing as well as the making alive, the wounding as well as the healing. And there is no escaping Me!" Who knows good and evil, after all? Who can comprehend why, in the wisdom of God, a fallen world *must* be afflicted with wars, injustice, poverty, crime, catastrophe, tears, and death, or why God will not allow the wise strategies of men to turn the world into paradise, or why God's children and heirs should be called upon to accept their full share and more of such "evil"? Yet the children know that the war God is waging is not finally against hunger and pain or against anything men regard as the "enemy." God's war is against man's ungodliness, against the cancer and gangrene of human nature, against all the deceit and evil that men try to disguise behind their fig leaves. And no man can comprehend or limit what God must do to wage that war, no matter how dreadful the "evil."

Is not this really what simple Christian piety has always known and confessed? It belongs to the paradox of our participation as saints in a world of sin that we live both *under* the knowledge of good and evil and yet *above* it. *Under* it we praise God for His blessings and flee to Him for refuge in every pain and distress. Under it we also see and respond to the grief and need of our neighbor. Yet we also pray, "Thy will be done on earth." By that prayer we rise *above* the knowledge of good and evil. We now surrender such distinctions and entrust the ultimate wisdom to our heavenly Father. That is not the prayer of the wise and prudent but of babes. It is the hardest prayer in the world to pray, yet what freedom and courage and peace and wisdom and power belong to those who have learned to pray it!

Now that is our Gospel. It comes to us in words. A theology that lies altogether under the knowledge of good and evil has little need of words, for it is natural to man. This Gospel, however, has to be told. Without words we cannot know it. Therefore the Biblical proclamation must not be cheapened, no matter what scandals it may raise for the humanistic piety of softhearted modern man.

There are many offenses. We have mentioned the modern hatred of monotheism and of original sin. But the doctrine of the church is also hated, that God should have a special, elect people, holy and separate from the world, who alone have hope and salvation and the knowledge of God.

With this the doctrine of the exclusiveness of Jesus Christ is hated. Nobody among the wise and prudent in our day wants to concede that one single event, involving this single Person, is so critically important that on the New Testament side of that event no knowledge of the living God and therefore no salvation is possible anywhere except through His name! The world scoffs at this, and even Christians find themselves squirming at the scoffing. Then they begin to stutter in their new and better wisdom that maybe it isn't really so, that Christ's death and resurrection must be only symbolic, that Christ is somehow majestically present wherever men strive to know God, that Christianity offers at best only a higher degree of clarity in the universal knowledge of God, that the incarnation of God in Christ is merely a paradigm for His incarnation in all His creatures. But if all this is so, why did that Man Jesus carry through that dreadful, lonely, and uncompromising battle in decisive opposition to the world as it was? Why does salvation require death, not Jesus' death only but the death of our whole natural self with all its wisdom and proud independence?

All such compromising robs Christ of His honor and sinners of their only hope and comfort. It cuts the heart out of the Bible, for if Christ is only a token of some kind, the cross is not necessary. Then nothing really happened there to destroy the world as it was and man as he is and to bring about a radically new creation. Then God is not a living God who sent His trusting Son into death and then raised Him up in everlasting triumph for our sakes. Then God is only an idea in the mind of man, and everybody has to find out whether he personally can find the idea in himself — and we are right back in relativism and lostness. And then the Word of God dies in the churches, for there is nothing to preach anymore, no beauty, no freedom, no life, no promise, no quiet, no hallelujah! Then the church cannot infect the world with life and holiness. The world has rather infected the church with its death and decay.

We who are Christ's holy people need to know this Jesus of ours better. We need to know the story of His Passion, why He died, what men had against Him, what made that death of His an atonement. We have to know why the

New Testament writers found themselves to be alive from the dead and in a new world once the hand of God was lifted from over the cleft of the rock in which His mercy had kept them hidden under darkness while He passed by. We have to be able to tell the story of what happened and to show clearly and in explicit words how every familiar and precious doctrine we have concerning Christ stands squarely on and in the death and resurrection history, in the conflict and terror and mighty drama of the terrible confrontation between God and His people that occurred in the Man called Jesus of Nazareth. We have to know better than ever why the Old Testament and the New Testament are one, why the New Testament writers quote the Old as fulfilled with such enthusiastic and crazy freedom that it sometimes looks as though the whole meaning of texts and contexts were being perverted.

We must know these things so that we can share more fully the riches of the Gospel and proclaim these events in their transforming power to create a hallelujah people — a people who know how to be free and to rest in their God, a people bound to one another in the community of love we call the holy church. We need to know these events so that we may rejoice in their eternal truth and through the Spirit of truth pass them on by Word and Sacrament from generation to generation. We need to know how it happens that those who share the sonship of Jesus by Baptism are freed from the fear of consequences and pursuit of advantages, freed to serve their Father and love their neighbor. Right there, in that story, in that dreadful fragment of human history, is the power to kill men as they are in order to raise them up to God's kind of life and hope and unity and peace.

But if it's history, it must come down to us by words. There's no getting around it. Somebody has to write or say the words. There is no Gospel without words, no sacrament either without words, no power and no Spirit without words. That's just the way it is with the Gospel. It is the foolishness of preaching that saves those who believe (1 Cor. 1:18 – 2:5). The words have to go out into all the earth and to the end of the world (Rom. 10:5-18). The feet that carry the servants of Christ over the mountains are most beautiful because they carry the mouth and tongue that will say the words.

Let's have no nonsense about a Gospel without words. There's another curious story hidden in the Book of Job. When the last of the calamities had struck Job down with miserable boils from head to toe, making him look a horrible mess, some friends came to visit and comfort him by showing their love to him. So they sat down around him silently, shaking their heads with sad expressions on their faces to convey their sympathy. And they tore their own clothes to show how they entered into his calamity, threw dust on their heads, and raised their voices and wept. They were willing to serve Job this way, and other ways too, if by doing so they could help him. They would gladly have brought him a cup of cold water or scratched him where he itched (with a stick at least, if not with their bare hands). They wanted him to know that they had not abandoned him. So they sat there by him, the friends did, seven days and seven nights, saying not a word. Presumably their actions should speak louder than words. Yet there is not the slightest evidence that Job found any comfort at all in the silent and sympathetic presence of his friends. On the contrary, when the seven days were over, Job had broken down completely. He was now perfectly ready to curse God and die. That was some mighty effective comfort his friends brought him, wasn't it!

But if our problem is that we haven't known the words, can we not ask God for them? "O Lord, open Thou my lips," we say (Ps. 51:15). He has to do the opening anyway. It's great to be free, though, free enough to rest in God our Father and engage Him in little conversations. Surely we are naked before Him; that's the great thing about it! We dare to be naked and not the least ashamed or defensive about it any more.

So talk to Him. Say: "Lord, my Father, Dona Hoffman's poem hits hard at me too. I'm so terribly inadequate at showing people Christ, and I've also known Him so little. And so I have this affliction, this stammering tongue. How on earth can I be any good to You?"

And your Father will say: "Yes, I know. But if you understood a little better about being a monotheist, you'd remember that among the other things I do, I also run the stammering-tongue concession and pass the things out the way I please—all the way from Moses to you. And you would relax a little and remember that I am also the God who opens blind eyes and deaf ears and makes the tongue of the dumb sing." (Ex. 4:10-12; Is. 35:3-6)

Let us worship that God of ours, therefore, let us talk to Him, trust Him, get to know Him. Let's get into His Bible so that the knowledge of the truth may expose whatever has to be exposed everywhere. Let the Word of God condemn the superficial and humanistic theological speculations on the liberal side, as well as the false fears, false reliances, false defenses on the conservative side. In our flesh we have compromised the faith with many subtle idolatries, but our Father has held us in spite of them, and He will hold us.

Stand on that Bible, and search out its meaning. Tear into it by every resource available, and make it speak to you. It is not a quick task and not easy. It demands a lifetime. But that Book still speaks, abundantly and powerfully. When it does, you will stand in awe and say, "Surely the Lord is in this Book!" You will see with your own eyes the riches of the glory of the backside of God. You will learn to rest in Him and to feed first your brothers and then the world with the bread of life. And as they eat they will join you in an uninhibited "Glory, hallelujah!" They will rejoice to know Christ and will gladly share Him. Never will they be ushered out as though "after the damning." For they will be nourished and grow up, in prosperity and in adversity, now and forever, by the peace of God that passes all understanding.

Then the holy infection will be at work in the body of humanity's death, to overcome and repel that death with the life of God in Christ. And the mercy of God will have its way in the world through "our Savior Christ Jesus, who abolished death and brought life and immortality to light through the Gospel." (2 Tim. 1:10)

Notes

1. Dietrich Bonhoeffer, *Schopfung und Fall* (Munich: Chr. Kaiser Verlag, 1937), trans. John C. Fletcher, *Creation and Fall* (London: SCM Press Ltd., 1959). Available in paperback, The Macmillan Company, New York, No. 08389. See at Gen. 2:17 and 3:4-6. Though Bonhoeffer has greatly enriched my own thinking at this point and many others, he does not pursue the implications of his definition in quite the way I do.

2. For Luther's "Heidelberg Disputation" in English, see the translation by Harold J. Grimm in *Luther's Works*, Vol. 31 (Philadelphia: Muhlenberg Press, 1957), pp. 39−70, especially Thesis 21 and its context. This thesis says: "A theology of glory calls evil good and good evil. A theology of the cross calls the thing what it actually is."

3. Thesis 20 of the "Heidelberg Disputation" reads: "He deserves to be called a theologian, however, who comprehends the visible and manifest things of God seen through suffering and the cross." "Manifest things of God" translates *posteriora dei,* namely that aspect of God (the backside) that He grants us to see. To look at the cross is to see what God has done in Christ. The contrast is with men's efforts to see "His invisible nature" (as in Rom. 1:20),

148

that is, to infer what God is like by looking at creation and by projecting large those human qualities that men regard as virtuous.

4. For a fuller development of this point, see my article "First Things First: The Question of Infant Communion," *Una Sancta*, XX, 4 (Advent 1963), 34 — 40. For a detailed study of the history and practice of Lutheran confirmation, see A. C. Repp, *Confirmation in the Lutheran Church* (St. Louis: Concordia Publishing House, 1964). See also Frank W. Klos, *Confirmation and First Communion*, published in 1968 by Augsburg Publishing House, Board of Publication of the Lutheran Church in America, and Concordia Publishing House.

Bibliography

Bertram, Robert W., ed. *The Lively Function of the Gospel.* St. Louis: Concordia Publishing House, 1967.

The Holy Bible

Bonhoeffer, Dietrich. *Schopfung und Fall.* Munich: Chr. Kaiser Verlag, 1937. Trans. John C. Fletcher, *Creation and Fall.* London: SCM Press Ltd., 1959. With *Versuchung.* Ed. Eberhard Bethge. Munich: Chr. Kaiser Verlag, 1953. Trans. Kathleen Downham, *Temptation.* New York: The Macmillan Company, 1965. Paperback 08389.

Bretscher, Paul G. *The World Upside Down or Right Side Up?* St. Louis: Concordia Publishing House, 1964.

_____. *Your Family — The Greatest Society.* St. Louis: Lutheran Laymen's League, 2185 Hampton Ave. 63139, 1966.

Caemmerer, R. R. *Feeding and Leading.* St. Louis: Concordia Publishing House, 1962.

Elert, Werner. *Das Christliche Ethos.* Tuebingen: Furche-Verlag, 1949. Trans. Carl J. Schindler, *The Christian Ethos.* Philadelphia: Muhlenberg Press, 1957.

Forsyth, P. T. *The Cruciality of the Cross*. Grand Rapids: Wm B. Eerdmans Publishing Company, 1966.

Franzmann, Martin, and Dean Lueking. *Grace Under Pressure*. St. Louis: Concordia Publishing House, 1966.

Keith-Lucas, Alan. *The Church and Social Welfare*. Philadelphia: The Westminster Press, 1962.

Koenker, Ernest B. *Worship in Word and Sacrament*. St. Louis: Concordia Publishing House, 1959.

Luther, Martin. *The Large Catechism*. In Theodore G. Tappert, ed., *The Book of Concord*. Philadelphia: Fortress Press, 1959.

Lutze, Karl. *To Mend the Broken*. St. Louis: Concordia Publishing House, 1964.

Marty, Martin E., ed. *Death and Birth of the Parish*. St. Louis: Concordia Publishing House, 1964.

Repp, Arthur C. *Confirmation in the Lutheran Church*. Saint Louis: Concordia Publishing House, 1964.

Schmemann, Alexander. *For the Life of the World*. New York: National Student Christian Federation, 475 Riverside Drive, 1963.

Shinn, Roger L. *Tangled World*. New York: Charles Scribner's Sons, 1965.

Simon, Arthur. *Faces of Poverty*. St. Louis: Concordia Publishing House, 1966.

Stählin, Wilhelm. *The Mystery of God.* Trans. R. B. Hoyle. St. Louis: Concordia Publishing House, 1964. German edition ca. 1937.

Stringfellow, William. *A Private and Public Faith.* Grand Rapids: Wm. B. Eerdmans Publishing Company, 1966.

Vicedom, Georg F. *Missio Dei.* Trans. Gilbert A. Thiele and Dennis Hilgendorf, *The Mission of God.* St. Louis: Concordia Publishing House, 1965.

_____. *Gebet fur die Welt.* Munich: Chr. Kaiser Verlag, 1965. Trans. Edward and Marie Schroeder, *Prayer for the World.* St. Louis: Concordia Publishing House, 1967.

Wingren, Gustaf. *Predikan.* Lund: C. W. K. Gleerup, 1949. Trans. Victor C. Pogue, *The Living Word.* Philadelphia: Muhlenberg Press, 1960.

Williams, Colin W. *Where in the World? Changing Forms of the Church's Witness.* New York: National Council of the Churches of Christ in the U. S. A., 475 Riverside Drive 10027, 1963.